For the men of Charlie Company, Second Battalion, Second Infantry Regiment, who shared this experience.

Edward Roby

HEAVY METAL

Memoir of a distant war

www.tredition.de

© 2020 Edward Roby

Verlag und Druck: tredition GmbH, Halenreie 40-44, Hamburg

ISBN
Paperback: 978-3-347-13049-4
Hardcover: 978-3-347-13050-0
E-Book: 978-3-347-13051-7

Cover design: Tamara Pirschalawa

Cover photograph: Soldiers of Company C, 2/2 Infantry, returning in column on their armored personnel carriers to Lai Khe base as pictured on First Infantry Division calendar page for October 1967.
Source: contribution from Willie C. Garner.

Contents

Introduction

Reflecting two decades ago on the yawning indifference of his cadets to the study of their army's role in Vietnam, a West Point instructor admitted: "I might as well be teaching the Peloponnesian Wars."

Col. Cole C. Kingseed's stinging remark on the shelf-life of military art rippled controversially through the news columns during the post-911 war fervor. If the colonel's subject looked quaint even then, why straggle in now with more ink on things that happened in Indochina at least 52 years ago? Hasn't it all been said?

History shelves are already full of good books on the Vietnam War. Courage, heroism, victories, even defeats have been duly memorialized in print. The authority of many exhaustively documented accounts is enhanced by eloquent prefaces from generals, politicians, historians – frequently adding their own abstract allusions to freedom, democracy and national greatness.

My collection of personal anecdotes lays no claim to such distinction. It began as a memoir, finally offering a frank response to the unspoken question: "What was it like in Vietnam, Grandpa?" That, at least, was the working title when I belatedly started to write. But the story took on a larger life of its own.

This narrative tracks the experience of Company C, 2nd Battalion, 2nd Infantry Regiment from late September 1967 through the end of April 1968. I was in command during that period, including the Tet offensive, so this small slice of our unit's history is treated from that vantage point.

The chapters roughly follow the chronological sequence of events. Exceptions are those on land mines, accidents, trouble shooting and daily life in the field camps – recurring themes illustrated with examples gathered from the entire tour. The last chapter, with an historian's retrospective, goes beyond the small world of Company C to shed critical light on the nature of this 30-year conflict.

As a mechanized – armored and mobile – infantry unit, we were somewhat rare in Vietnam. We probably spent more time in the field than the more common light infantry units, but they often saw more intense action when inserted by helicopter into contested spots. By contrast, we were so heavily armed that a prudent enemy had to look for softer targets. The greater threat to us and our armored vehicles was his land mines.

This account owes some important details to others. Prominent among them were our battalion commander, Lieutenant Colonel Henry L. Davisson, and the commander of our sister Company B, Captain George "Sonny" Gratzer, both now deceased. Retired Col. James Perlmutter, who had served with us as a senior medic, supplied many a forgotten fact and was a source of encouragement for my project. My wife, Margarete, kindly helped with proof reading. And I remain most grateful to my guardian angel, who has never taken a day off.

The narrative's actors are mostly identified by their radio call-signs in lieu of proper names and titles because that was the way we usually addressed one another. Another reason to dispense with names is that I am working from memory. My field notebooks went missing in the course of eleven subsequent career moves on three continents. But scenes etched in vivid memory aided recall of the described actions. For the uninitiated, a glossary of military terms of art is included.

Around two thousand names are engraved on a First Infantry Division monument in a small park behind the Blair House, half a block off Pennsylvania Avenue in Washington, D.C. This memorial to the division's Vietnam War dead honors at least a dozen men who were with me in Company C, which also counted its wounded in the high double digits.

This is a story of a company of men with little in common who came to trust even their lives to one another. Thrust into hazardous circumstances, these companions answered the call of duty and contributed admirably to our mutual purpose – especially the will to survive. Their youthful enthusiasm, curiosity, energy and inborn gift of humor steeled them against daunting hardships.

It's often said that war is hell. Yet warfare stubbornly stands forth in human history as the recurring hallmark of what we call civilization. Friend or foe, those lucky enough to look back on such an early crucible of experience often cherish it as the greatest adventure of their lifetime. That alone makes our tale worth telling.

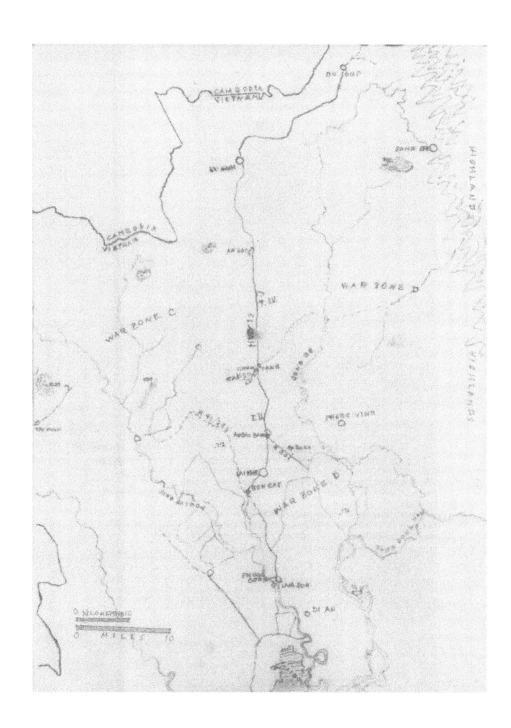

9

Chapter 1

Shenandoah II

Know your enemy, know yourself. You will win a hundred battles. The ancient martial wisdom may work well against Viet Cong in the bush. But Sun Tzu neglected to mention another possibility: The first "battle" for a newly minted commander could also pit him against an enemy in disguise – the ambitious lieutenant standing right behind him.

A captain in command of an infantry company is backed up by a first lieutenant, the right-hand man called an executive officer (XO). But it happens every so often that this same senior lieutenant had already been serving as acting company commander in the interregnum before his new captain arrived.

That could cause friction if the junior officer deeply resents the revised command arrangement as a de facto demotion. So it was with my first XO, who was loathe to relinquish his authority over the company just because a new boss with two silver bars of rank had been installed.

Two bighorn rams in rut would have settled the matter of primacy pronto, the bigger one butting the other straight off an alpine cliff. But the unspoken challenge from my second in command was a gentlemen's battle of wits. A subtle tug-o-war over who should be calling the shots in Charlie Company flickered for roughly the first ten days of my tenure as commanding officer.

My lieutenant was confident, well spoken and assertive. He already knew the platoon leaders and key personnel, having basked in his temporary role as their leader. Never openly disloyal, he also never skipped a chance to remind the company of his own authority, issuing all sorts of "valuable" guidance, often in my name.

By contrast, I was the greenhorn. I still hadn't had to duck that fabled "shot fired in anger", the real rite of passage for a combat infantry commander. While learning the ropes, I also needed to rely on the support of my seasoned executive officer. That's perfectly normal. But this change of command was less than smooth.

About two days after my arrival, our battalion struck its defensive base west of Phuoc Vinh on the Song Be river in War Zone D. We were going to join a corps-sized operation called Shenandoah II in the Long Nguyen Secret Zone near a Michelin plantation to the northwest. The mission of the First Infantry Division and the Twenty-Fifth Infantry Division was to cut VC/NVA infiltration and supply lines running toward Saigon from the Ho Chi Minh Trail coming out of Cambodia. The enemy's main staging area was this thickly forested bulge of War Zone C.

Light infantry battalions were already converging by helicopter on assigned positions in this war zone. The Second Battalion, Second Infantry Regiment punched into the operation from the southeast, making an uppercut starting at Ben Cat, just northeast of the Iron Triangle and Saigon River, Being a mechanized unit, we then headed northward along still usable portions of an old French laterite trace, Road 240, or 41 on our maps, camping initially near the last hamlet before the declared free-fire zone.

The villagers took no notice of us. Children frolicked outside the slightly elevated thatch-roofed houses, ignoring the cobras hunting rats under their homes – a fascinating and practical symbiosis. Cleaning our newly issued M-16 rifles had become the command obsession. Too often they tended to jam from all the dust and mud. Platoon sergeants preferred the lighter, semi-automatic AR-15 version that somehow seemed to work better, at least until the M-16 was reissued with 10 design improvements. To be on the safe side, some soldiers swpped the new rifles for reliable old M-14s.

In the ebb and flow of the decades-old Indochina conflict, Road 41 had been repeatedly mined and de-mined, sabotaged and repaired again. Here and there, excavated tiger-tooth obstacles still detoured tracks and wheeled vehicles around strategic bottlenecks. But the route north was now generally passable, which was no special favor to us. NVA units and equipment heading toward Saigon were certainly using it as a transit corridor.

Lorraine II

Moving ahead, our lead element discovered a hand poking up from the soil beside the road. Attached to a VC body, it qualified as an initial body count. Alpha Company and the battalion headquarters established their next base a dozen miles to the north. Bravo and Charlie companies did the same further up the road. We shared our first base camp, called Lorraine II, with a 105-mm howitzer battery lifted in by workhorse helicopters. The surrounding forest was full of VC/NVA and their camps, tunnels, caches and trails. They watched our every move. Daily sniping or small gunfights would soon cost Charlie Company at least half a dozen casualties.

I spent the daylight hours with my three rifle platoons looking for trouble in the woods. My executive officer looked after logistics, supply, personnel and administrative tasks back in our night defensive position. The clear division of functions left little room for ego-driven grandstanding, although my XO had already gotten on the wrong side of Bravo's CO by evicting one of his squads from a position he claimed as ours.

One afternoon my executive officer crossed a red line. He saw fit to radio my line platoon leaders with some operating instructions – combat operations being my command prerogative. In another age, that might have brought forth the dueling pistols. When my temper cooled, I realized that this gratuitous gaffe handed me carte blanche to clean house.

I also keyed the company radio net. When all platoon leaders had responded, I revoked any and all orders they may have been given. I told them a time to report to my command track in the evening to receive the order of operations from their commanding officer, Charlie Six. The next morning a helicopter transported my Charlie Five with a bruised ego back to the battalion base camp to await reassignment.

Battalion headquarters routinely monitors all company networks, so no one was surprised at the blowout in Charlie Company. It created an opportune time for other big changes already in the air. Daring Six, the battalion commander, simultaneously replaced his own operations officer with a more able major. The battalion sergeant major seized the occasion to fire my first sergeant, in whom he lacked confidence. My new executive officer and new first sergeant proved highly professional. Both stayed with me for the next seven months.

Meanwhile, in the other war, the enemy was standing his ground for a change. The intensity of combat was building toward bigger engagements in this part of the war zone. This was toward the end of the wet monsoon that had brought daily rains since the spring. The light infantry battalions were all in position, probing day and night for the main enemy formations. Finding them was inevitable, given the sheer concentration of U.S. troops maneuvering around the Michelin.

The secret zone was heavily wooded and drained by small streams. Patrols and listening posts around our base weren't enough to suppress brazen VC snipers in the forest. A Soviet-designed B-40 rocket launcher fired down from a tree just outside our perimeter blasted a hole in a track gunner's armored hatch copula, inflicting a gory gut wound on the gunner. No one expected to see him again. The light 40-mm VC anti-tank weapon, also called RPG-2, was recoilless, portable and lethal.

The next day, a VC marksman concealed in a spider hole picked off a soldier in one of my patrols before it had advanced a hundred yards outside the base. The unlucky private first class was our first combat fatality on my watch. We never could find the spider hole or the shooter.

After sorting out the tactical situation, I asked my new first sergeant about finding a replacement. He'd already beaten me to it. Toward evening there was a quiet ceremony in the NDP. We gathered around the fallen soldier's rifle, bayonet fixed and thrust in the ground vertically upside down, his helmet placed on top of the rifle butt. A few words were spoken. We returned to our routine, each with his own thoughts.

Late one evening, a three-man listening post about fifty meters outside our western wire called to say it was not alone in the forest. It was hearing strange noises, something moving around them in the undergrowth. Their next radio call reported more of the same. VC? Maybe not, they said. Some animal? Yes, they were now pretty sure they were being stalked by a tiger. Are you locked and loaded? Yes, but we can't see anything, although the growls are getting closer. No one was eaten that night. After dawn a patrol searched the LP's location. There were plenty of prints, including VC. The presence of a big cat couldn't be confirmed – or ruled out.

Charlie and Bravo conducted daily dismounted sweeps through thick woods, following assigned compass headings. Progress was glacial, visibility curtailed. To avoid ambush, we'd stop our advance every so often to "cloverleaf". The flanking platoons of the company's triple column would send scouts out to the left or right; the platoon in middle would send men to the front and rear.

After crawling through a bamboo thicket one day, we reached a wide rice paddy at the edge of a woods. The easy way forward was to walk atop the paddy dike. Two long antennae made my command group with its RTOs a prime target. A couple of bursts of automatic fire kicked up the dirt at our feet. The shooting came out of a wood line on the opposite side of the paddy.

This was a new experience for some of our men, who were slow to take cover and return fire. I pegged a few rounds toward the shooters, knowing that my .45 was practically as harmless as a slingshot beyond 50 feet. About the same time, Bravo Company took three casualties in a nearby firefight.

Bravo's contact reports on the battalion network immediately attracted a command & control helicopter. This C&C was that of the deputy division commander, call-sign Danger 79. Dropping a smoke grenade to mark a landing spot for a medical evacuation helicopter, he told Bravo to go there pronto. Urgent guidance continued when the company failed to move fast enough to suit the man in the sky. Yet the soldiers, scarcely visible from the air, were carrying wounded men on makeshift stretchers while cutting paths through impenetrable brush that only machetes could clear.

Exasperated, Bravo Six finally keyed the net, snapping that he could run his company if he could just get off radio. Pausing to digest that, the general signed off, "I understand, son. Carry on." Capt. George "Sonny" Gratzer, Bravo Six, became a battalion legend for asserting his command prerogative as the unit leader on the ground. The sources of annoying radio static from the sky came to be derided as "flying squad leaders."

Yet the commander on the spot isn't always privvy to the bigger picture. I had a brush with my boss, call-sign Daring Six, when he check-fired my mortars and told me to break off a pursuit that looked promising. As he later explained, marching to the sound of the guns would have taken us

14

into a sister battalion's AO where we would likely have tangled with their reconnaissance patrol.

The battalion commander also recommended we go mounted for a change. Having avoided taking the APCs on sweeps into such soggy, heavily wooded terrain, I soon found that they actually performed quite well. Our M113A1's were powered by 215-hp Detroit Diesel engines, unlike the gasoline-driven version that caused me constant maintenance headaches in Germany. The new tracks would simply mow down small trees, making Charlie Company's mounted sweeps faster and deeper. I also quit directing my maneuvering vehicles with hand signals when the boss opined that standing atop my command track, gripping an antenna for balance, made me too inviting a target.

Looking on foot for a suspected encampment one day, the Second Platoon drew fire from a wood line. I joined them as the lead squad entered the trees. The point man froze in mid-stride, pointing to a large circular object standing head high on a wooden tripod. It looked like a white cyclopse-eye the size of a wagon-wheel pizza. This homemade claymore mine went off almost simultaneously, spraying hot chunks of jagged scrap metal. An unseen enemy had detonated it by electric wire. This was the base camp. An elaborate underground complex suggested a unit headquarters. We followed a blood trail.

Close by was the entrance to a long tunnel that must have served as a field hospital. We recovered assorted items of equipment and a trove of pharmaceuticals and surgical kit. Our paramedics put the captured medicines in a sandbag that was sent on to division intelligence. They were keen to know what foreign countries were supplying the enemy with sophisticated medical equipment. We rigged the tunnel complex with C-4 charges, demolishing whatever we couldn't take with us.

On another sweep a VC anti-armor team with an RPG scored a hit on a track. The Third Platoon leader, Lt. Willie Ruffin, was among the wounded. Brave and taciturn, he recovered to rejoin us within a week. My new executive officer was also sidelined a couple of days – by a scorpion. It stung him twice in the back of the neck inside his M-114 track. Why the critter was lurking so high up on a radio wall mounting as the XO leaned back his head made for a bit of a mystery.

We also lost our most experienced mortar gunner, a tall sergeant known as "Slim", to a disabling freak accident during a fire mission. On balance, though, the enemy seemed less than eager to face down our oncoming armored vehicles and heavy machine guns. A few light infantry units were less favored. One of them was the Second Battalion, 28th Infantry.

Death Trap

That outfit was ambushed and destroyed just southwest of us on Oct. 17, 1967. The engagement entered military annals as the Battle of Ong Thanh. Apart from stateside news dispatches and the official military accounts, more than one book* covers this battle. I mention it here because Charlie and Bravo companies happened to be four kilometers from the scene, making us perhaps the nearest fresh infantry that could have been sent as a relief column. Instead, our soldiers were detailed to pass in daisy chain a steady flow of ammunition to the 105-mm howitzers firing in support of the doomed battalion.

We followed the fighting on both the infantry and artillery radio networks. My map reconnaissance showed three small streams to be crossed between us and them. I issued a warning order to my platoons. One after another, the embattled battalion and company nets fell silent as their command groups fell under deadly fire from bunkers and from the trees. As we listened, two wounded artillery forward observers trying gamely to direct supporting fires, their voices weakening to raspy whispers as they bled to death.

Lieutenant Colonel Terry de la Mesa Allen Jr., the 2/28th commander, was the son of a World War II commanding general of the First Infantry Division. His battalion, call-sign Dauntless, entered the 17 Oct. ambush with just two half-strength rifle companies after a couple of off-target airstrikes and without precise artillery preparation on a probable enemy concentration. The division later called Ong Thanh a "meeting engagement."

An intelligence fix passed to our battalion and included in my boss' order to me and Bravo Six the evening of Oct. 16 went into our field notes: "Multi-battalion base camp 500 men heavily armed 2 K's north" of Lorraine I. That pretty much pegged the ambush site on Ong Thanh stream. Try to imagine Scotland Yard using the term meeting engagement to explain a victim's last encounter with Jack the Ripper.

My boss knew Allen from their West Point days. A quarter century after Ong Thanh I chanced to ask Daring Six what went wrong. They marched into the forest on the same heading three days running, he said bluntly. In plain words, time enough for the larger NVA/VC unit to prepare a perfect killing zone. And why weren't we committed? It was a sister brigade's operation; they chose to handle it themselves, he said.

When Shenandoah II ended, our battalion headed south on the same road. The dead hand was still sticking out of the ground, having probably boosted some unit's body count again. We camped once more near the hamlet with the cobras. In the evening an ambush patrol surprised some VC. Our mortars fired in support. Short round! shouted the chief of a gun crew. A listening post barely a hundred yards outside the wire radioed for help: two men, badly hurt. A medical evacuation was requested. The helicopter pilot refused to fly there without a secure landing zone. Time elapsed. Another chopper agreed to land. Two men from the listening post died in route to hospital.

The short round was eventually blamed on old munition stocks with powder charges that had been wet at one point. A directive was issued against using anything more than one bag of propellant charge on the projectile fins, limiting the infantry company mortars to one quarter of their range.
—

* A richly detailed account of that battle is found in *They Marched into Sunlight* by David Maraniss (Simon & Schuster, New York, 2003)

Chapter 2

Mines and Men

Our usual daylight mission was to "Search & Destroy." Even this martial term of art conveyed a subtle admission that we seldom knew where the enemy was. But it often took on a more sardonic meaning for my mechanized infantrymen, the modern version of foot soldiers on horseback.

We'd search ever so diligently for the elusive Viet Cong until we "found" one of their land mines. That phase ends with a bang; a VC mine protests explosively when run over by an unwary 11-ton M-113 armored personnel carrier, called an A-Cav, APC, PC or just a track. Our S&D areas concealed hundreds of VC mines – improvised, hybrid, manufactured, small anti-personnel, big anti-tank, pressure-detonated or remotely trigger on cue with hidden wires. If we had had enough men and tracks, I suppose we could have found them all.

The most common scenario went like this: The disturbed land mine obligingly destroys itself, putting the unlucky tracked vehicle out of action with a broken hard-rubber track shoe or mangled steel tread. The explosion simultaneously catapults a squad of soldiers right off the top of the track. Arms or ribs occasionally fracture when men land akimbo on the ground. The rest of the unit takes up security positions, smokes cigarettes and waits.

The odds of a combat vehicle becoming an impromptu mine sweeper mimick Russian roulette. Given the routine risk of hitting mines, each track carries versatile maintenance tools and several sections of spare tread draped over the vehicle's frontal wooden trim-vane. The typical jungle repair work – if no one was hurt badly – would idle the whole column for about half an hour.

The daily hazard of buried, pressure-detonated land mines made the official acronym APC (armored personnel carrier) a bit of a misnomer. Trusting their own flak jackets instead, our soldiers always perched precariously on top of their moving combat vehicles, never inside where the thoughtful manufacture had provided fold-down canvass-covered benches to seat nine or ten men.

The track driver was the odd man out. He had his own interior throne in front of the steering laterals, pedals and engine controls. His exclusive compartment was capped by a heavy protective hatch cover, usually left wide opened for good reason. A standard land mine, about the size and shape of a kid's birthday cake, might cause the driver no more than a headache if it detonated underneath a tread. But there were other kinds of mines capable of blasting him skyward like a Polaris missile leaving a silo – unless his skull had smashed on a closed, armored hatch cover.

To one of those devilish others I probably owed my own coveted command slot in the mechanized 2nd Battalion, 2nd Infantry Regiment – the 2/2 Inf. The battalion was short two captains. An unexploded 8-inch artillery round re-jiggered as a blockbuster anti-tank mine and planted in the mechanized line of march had just killed a new commander of Bravo Company along with his track crew. That had happened 14 Sept. 1967, ten days before a helicopter dropped me off at the battalion's field location overlooking the ruined hamlet of Ap Bo La on the fringe of War Zone D.

Another new captain had already reported for duty a week before me. On the spot he was made the next commander of the unlucky unit. The battalion commander gave him a curt directive: "Bravo Company has a morale problem. Fix it." Decades after the unforgettable mine incident at a notorious road intersection dubbed Claymore Corners, Company B's veterans still shared vivid memories of how the 14 Sept. blast had changed their perception of buried risks.

"Our Track #221 was at the head of the column. Myself and three others were assigned to mine-sweep the raised section of roadway... not long after Captain Rose's PC was blown," one soldier wrote in an exchange on his unit's veterans forum with the company commander (CO) who fixed the morale problem.

"We were, to say at the least, taking our time, as we probed every metallic signal we picked up over our headsets. Apparently, back in the column, you were getting a little antsy, because our squad leader ... hollered down to us that we were taking too long. My response to [him] was that I had no problem with stepping back and letting the CO bring his track up to be the first across, but I'll be damned if I was going say all was clear, and climb back on 221 to be the first across (or not), just because some new F_ _ _k'n CO was in a hurry. Needless to say, we finished sweeping at our own pace. No more was said, and no mines were detected."

The CO replied. "Yes, we were all hollered at for moving too slow. You guys had it easy coming from me. I had to contend with some heavies coming down on me, but I knew the right rate of march and accepted it all. After all, after Joe Rose died, a week later I nearly bought it myself only yards (but off the road) from where Joe blew up. Lt. Hank Baxter got me to stop my track, having noticed a rubber dish upside down right next to our tread. We backed off slowly and blew the damn thing, leaving a crater ten feet deep and nearly twenty feet across. Imagine the mess that would have made, and my wife and mother would have felt bad."

The 2/2 knew this mine-studded location as Bau Bang, the name of a ruined village that still existed only on our maps. I got there in late September. I was a greenhorn captain, newly arrived in Vietnam. Knowing that I had led a mech platoon on a previous tour in Germany, the 2/2's commanding lieutenant colonel – radio call sign: Daring Six – promptly put me in charge of Company C, one of his three combat maneuver elements.

For the next seven plus months I was Daring Charlie Six, the radio call sign of the commander of Company C. Our 2/2 Infantry battalion – radio call sign: Daring – had the distinction of being the only mechanized outfit among the ten infantry battalions of the First Infantry Division – call sign: Danger. Our battalion packed a particularly heavy punch. The division made sure to keep us always up to authorized (TO&E) strength.

For Charlie Company, that was 189 soldiers and fleet of 16 APCs, each mounting a formidable .50 caliber machine gun. A couple of light tanks borrowed from an armored unit were usually part of our team. We also had a weapons platoon with 90-millimeter recoiless anti-tank rifles and three 81-millimeter mortar tubes. My executive officer, Charlie Five, had a compact M-114 track with a light machine gun. A mess crew, paramedics and others looking after logistics and administrative chores rounded out the fielded entourage.

We rarely visited our rear base in Lai Khe. Home was War Zones C and D between the river Song Be and Song Dong Nai river on the East and the Michelin Plantation to the West plus the fields, paddies and hamlets around the Iron Triangle and Lam Son south of Lai Khe. The company spent its nights in defensive perimeters we hastily built for ourselves or in existing fire bases shared with other units. By day, my three rifle platoons were out with me on the prowl, either mounted or on foot. One might say there was a tacit understanding: We ruled our part of Vietnam in daylight; the VC owned the night.

Given a choice, my mounted soldiers would have much preferred a rousing shootout with the Viet Cong to the next encounter with their insidious mines. These were easily our worst enemy. The outcome of one jinxed operation near the village of Phuoc Quang in the Lam Son district northeast of the division rear base at Di An speaks volumes.

Working a Minefield

First, a brief epilogue: About 35 year after that bizarre action, a stranger tracked me down in Europe. Our regimental association had shared with him my most recent coordinates. His e-mail message established that I had been his father's commanding officer in Vietnam. He sought a first-hand account of what had happened to his dad. He was the only son of Sgt. Adams, a name I hadn't forgotten.

The father was a married National Guardsman, part of an emergency levy called to active duty during the war. A model soldier, he had earned his Combat Infantry Badge for finishing a month in our unit on the very same day he was killed. "I wrote a letter of condolence through official channels to your mother. You've never seen it?" I asked. The son reminded me that he was just an infant at the time and that his mother must have put the letter away in her personal papers: "I never saw my father. I know him only from what others remembered." I told him the story:

Adams was a squad leader walking directly in front of me through a dense thicket until a grenade went off during a 1968 operation near Lam Son. We were advancing silently from east to west in three single files, hoping to surprise a VC/NVA unit. Extreme precaution was taken, since we already knew this place to be a vertical minefield. The point man had almost reached a relatively safe clearing when he or someone else disturbed a French potato-masher grenade wired to a sapling.

The booby trap didn't make much of a bang, so I was surprised to see Adams crumble slowly to the ground. No clear sign of a wound or gushing blood was evident. A shard of shrapnel must have flown through his parted lips, piercing the carotid artery inside the throat. A medic who picked his way gingerly forward along the immobilized file detected no pulse. Six of us maneuvered the fallen sergeant to the rear on an improvised stretcher of ponchos. A dust-off helicopter quickly landed in the dry rice paddy where our sweep had started. It was way too late.

That was the belated end of our three-day operation in this same area toward the end of January 1968. It had begun with urgent intelligence that an enemy regiment had infiltrated Lam Son and fortified the woods and cluster of villages separating Lai Khe from Saigon's northern suburbs. Our brigade's mission was to drive them out with a couple of battalions. We were holding a long string of night defensive positions to the north, the 2/2 on the left, Charlie Company on its left flank. Each unit was then assigned a different infantry objective. Ours wasn't much bigger than three or four football fields.

Dismounting ahead of a heavy jungled barrier on Day One, we began to search on foot. There was no sign of VC. But concealed booby traps soon sidelined a couple of men with shrapnel wounds. My First Platoon leader, Lt. Dave Stanley, was a casualty. Then a squad leader impaled his right leg by falling onto sharpened bamboo stakes in a punji pit disguised with brush cover. Our sweep of the whole area found neither VC nor their base camp.

Day Two dawned with mortars and 105-millimeter howitzers softening up our infantry objective. Intelligence insisted the enemy was present, probably operating from a network of underground tunnels. Our infantry sweep initially discovered two shallow VC graves. We were ordered to dig up the bodies. Even before the first putrescent cadaver was unearthed, the repulsive stench of death forced my digging detail to cover their noses with masks of wet handkerchiefs. Although the graves were several days old, we could at least report a body count.

Grave desecration stopped abruptly when more booby traps exploded. Finding a hidden trail, the headstrong chief medic manueuvered his track toward the injured men – his own bad idea. Suddenly, there was an ear-splitting detonation. Like a giant frisby, the 50-pound armored hatch cover of this APC swished past my head at warp speed, an instant before the explosion's shock wave knocked us all flat. The heavy M-113 had somersaulted in mid air, coming to rest topside down.

The unconscious driver was upside-down in his compartment, the crown of his head now showing an inch or two from the ground. Barely breathing, he could only be extracted head-first by digging a meter-deep recess under the inverted track. We set to work with entrenching tools but the ground seemed hard as concrete. The medics were retrieved from the woods a dozen meters away, all of them suffering broken limbs and contusions. They would not be coming back. The battalion later risked its cherry-picker track recovery vehicle to right the mangled APC and tow it out of the minefield.

Day Three opened with a more thorough preparatory bombardment from 4.2-inch heavy mortars and 155-millimeter division artillery. We hoped that would clear some of the mines and booby traps by triggering secondary explosions. The brigade was still spoiling for a body count. This time approaching from the east instead of the north, my infantry started the sweep that ended in the thicket with the fatal French grenade.

If this were a contest of attrition, the rising casualty count weighed in the enemy's favor: One squad leader dead; an evacuated track driver not expected to live; one platoon leader and two more squad leaders among the seven or eight other men sidelined with wounds. Against that tally, we had only the decomposing corpses of two VC who had probably fallen in some earlier fight. Not a shot was fired during the whole operation; there was nothing to shoot at. Charlie Company never flushed out a single live VC or NVA, let alone a purported regiment of them.

My battalion commander tacitly agreed with me that yet another stroll through this vertical minefield would be counterproductive. But it must have taken his very best powers of persuasion to make that case stick at brigade headquarters. We pulled out to try our luck elsewhere.

There was an eerie logic to the absence of enemies. Experience had made the VC astute observers of habitual U.S. Army movements and responses. Had some cunning leader lured us into a trap, knowing that one never interrupts an adversary hell bent on making a mistake? The Vietnamese had already defeated the French. Maybe a sliver of the same tactical savvy once so famously distilled by Napoleon had just been turned on us by an upstart VC commander. Ironic, but not unthinkable.

Mines and Vibes

Mines become an obsession. When the risk was greatest, particularly when a resupply convoy was scheduled to pass on Thunder Road, I'd first detail infantrymen with mine sweepers. They would proceed three or four abreast down Highway 13, sweeping before them practically every square inch of surface in 90-degree arcs. Their headsets would pick up any telltale electronic signals from the discus-shape metal detectors attached to the bottom of long probes fitted with handles. Road intersections were especially suspect.

Precaution was abandoned in combat emergencies. It wasn't even possible when we drove our tracks through fields and forest, which was most of the time. Engineer Rome plows had cleared strips of 30 to 50 meters on both sides of Thunder Road and a couple of the side roads. If we had reason to suspect mining, we'd shun the road and drive through the limbs and branches littering the cleared shoulders. Wise to this ploy, the VC learned to place mines there too. They didn't even trouble themselves to bury the mines because branches concealed them anyway.

I gradually developed a knack for land mine detection. On one S&D mission in open woods south of Road 301, our mounted column was searching fresh trails used by VC or NVA. We broke into a small clearing where two faint trails intersected, just as my map reconnissance had revealed. If I were a VC, I thought, this barely visible junction would be the place I'd mine. Noticing that one of my two M48A tanks from Bravo Co, 4/64 Armor was about to rumble right over that spot, I keyed the company net in alarm. The blast cut me off in mid-transmission.

Brushing the dust and dirt off his spattered fatigues, the platoon sergeant in charge of the tank section remarked: "Who'd have thought we'd hit a mine here in the middle of nowhere?" One tread was a goner but no one was hurt. We needed to summon the battalion cherry picker to retrieve that tank.

A new second lieutenant joined us in April. I positioned my command track with his platoon during an S&D that took down us down the 301 road again. Prudently shunning the roadbed, we moved through the deadfall on the cleared shoulder. Glancing at the platoon leader's track moving straight ahead on my left front, an uncanny foreboding gripped me. I keyed the radio net to tell him to veer away, *now*. If he even heard his call-sign, it was instantly drowned out by the mine explosion. His arm was broken, his crew writhing on the ground.

Word got around, probably first among the track drivers, about the Old Man's sixth sense with buried mines. The unrelenting weight of responsibility for lives and equipment over several months may be enough to sharpen a commander's natural instinct for imminent danger. Yet, inert inanimate objects like mines radiate neither morphic nor psychic fields to betray their malign presence. Why then the sudden flashes of highly focused intitution that prove explosively correct? I've never found a rational explanation.

My 25th birthday passed quietly in the field 13 days before Tet. The Army would typically replace infantry company commanders at half-year intervals, if they hadn't been dusted off sooner. Other officers were always waiting for their own unit command slots. In the 2/2, I got Charlie Company almost the same time my friend took over Bravo Company. He was evacuated with multiple gunshot wounds the end of February. The Alpha Company commander, chosen from battalion staff, was also shot up early in Tet after leading his unit for less than two months. I somehow managed to outlast all other COs on line.

After a one-week R&R respite in Hong Kong the start of April, I was actually looking forward to keeping my company until the end of my tour. Toward end of April, I received orders transferring me to brigade staff in Lai Khe in May. My new job was assistant to the S3 operations officer. Maybe the change was just in time.

The rumor mill let me follow the movements of my old unit for nostalgia's sake. Word got around Lai Khe in late June: Charlie Company's new commander was among the casualties of an operation conducted a few miles east of the division base. His APC was blown up by an 8-inch artillery round rigged as a mine. I'd never met the man. But I was saddened to hear that my replacement was barely alive, having lost both legs and more.

His track would have been my lucky old APC, #306. Under my command it had a distinction – the only line track in the company that hadn't hit a mine. The odds against that were about 14:1. I wanted to believe that my able driver, Sp4 Guadeloupe, had already completed his year and rotated safely back to the States.

—

Chapter 3

'Commie' Mosquitoes

My own mechanized infantry company somehow became ground zero in a mysterious, unprecedented and highly unwelcome biomedical drama that initially threatened to leave yawning gaps in the strategic U.S. military cordon around Saigon. It was our Charlie Company that sparked off what one wag dubbed the "communist mosquito" attack on the First Infantry Division.

The crisis erupted suddenly in November 1967 while we were conducting daily search-and-destroy sweeps of War Zone C around our night defensive position (NDP), one of the division's string of fortified "Thunder" bases astride Highway 13 between Lai Khe and the Cambodian border. Here's what happened:

One evening, as I'm giving my operations order to the platoon leaders, 1Lt. O'Reilly, my executive officer, or second in command (i.e. XO, call-sign: Daring Charlie Five), excuses himself, pleading acute suffering from a splitting headache and bouts of delirium. In the next few days, a solid one-third of the company – morning report strength: 189 men – came down with the same symptom: dangerously high fever. We had to pour cool water over their heads when the thermometer reading threatened to top 105. These soldiers became literally immobilized, flat on their backs and quite obviously "combat ineffective".

This was way beyond sick call. All of these men had to be evacuated quickly to the rear for special malaria treatment that must have saved some lives. This heretofore unfamiliar form of the prevalent tropical disease unfolded in three clinical phases, each about a week long. The result was that dozens of my soldiers were sidelined for three weeks. The star-frocked great ones were not pleased. I very nearly got relieved of command over this outbreak. After all, it had been designated a command responsibility to ensure that every man in the unit swallowed his flat yellow malaria pill handed out by the paramedic as they passed through the morning chow line. The unit commander was required to observe this ritual. The fact that my unit had suddenly been more than decimated by malaria was taken as a sign of dereliction of the duty to see that the soldiers were taking their anti-malaria drug: *Quod erat demonstrandum.*

That snap verdict was overtaken by events: Right after mine, a couple of nearby Thunder NDPs and firebases were also laid low with the same virulent malaria symptoms. And the reports from the medical rear quickly established that this form of malaria they were now seeing in us was quite different from the local kind here in Cochin that was prevented completely by the big yellow pill. This new scourge was identified as falciparum malaria, which was endemic only in the northern region of Vietnam. So, how did it get here?

The medical findings shifted the spotlight of suspicion away from supposedly negligent company commanders. So, the revised theory was that newly arrived NVA units coming down the Ho Chi Minh Trail through Laos and Cambodia were now operating in the woods around us. The female Anopheles mosquitoes would draw their nightly meals of blood from NVA soldiers who were previously infected in the North with the Plasmodium falciparum parasite from Tonkin or Annam. Then the same mosquitoes would make their short buzz over to bite our guys, too.

To impudent female mosquitoes, red-blooded Americans were apparently just as tasty as their traditional Indochinese menu. And the nasty parasites they carried with them had no ethnic preference among human hosts. That revised theory of propinquity was rendered entirely plausible when an NVA battalion attacked our position one night a few weeks later. And then the Tet offensive broke out the end of January 1968.

The P. falciparum parasite supposedly causes around half of all the world's malaria cases. It is also the most deadly parasitic form, responsible for nearly all the human malarial fatalities. The report of the World Health Organization for 2019, for example, estimated 228 million cases of malaria worldwide in 2018, resulting in an estimated 405,000 deaths, now mostly in Africa.

P. falciparum is also linked to a subsequent blood cancer, called Burkitt's lymphoma, and is classified as a carcinogen. Genetic researchers claim that this vicious mosquito-borne critter must have made the leap to humans from a gorilla some ten thousand years ago. But the incubation period after the bite of a carrier mosquito is only a matter of days.

Black Pill

The Army's answer to the P. falciparum malarial outbreak was a second mandatory pill, this time a little black one. The black pill's active ingredient was certainly a chloroquine varient, perhaps hydroxychloroquine. It may have been the forerunner of commercial mefloquine hydrochloride, a widely used anti-malaria compound now in disrepute. That drug was first developed by the U.S. Army in a research crash program launched in 1963 and focused on Vietnam. The Army plunged into its own pharmaceutical development when it noticed that the available malaria drugs were often ineffective. But the new black pill worked; the ground war could continue as planned.

Yet chloroquine or mefloquine HCL have proven a mixed blessing for some veterans in two respects, one pretty obvious, the other arguably scandalous. First of all, some men just despised the pills because they caused diarrhea. And after Tet some draftees plucked out of a society that was turning against the war may have harbored another, tacit objection to pill-popping. After all, catching falciparum malaria could be a lucky ticket home.

That I also have from a friend, an enlisted Marine infantryman who lost a leg to multiple gunshot wounds during his 1968-1969 combat tour. The Marines rigidly enforced the same morning pill-taking ritual. And the high command elevated this to a high priority partly because it was aware of the pills' unpopularity in the ranks.

Secondly, anti-malaria drugs have side-effects. The same ex-Marine, who became a civilian entrepreneur in the health-care profession, added this twist: "We heard that when they were dispensing this medication in 1968-69 that we were being used as the human experimental phase of the FDA drug certification program." The checkered history of mefloquine lends some credence to that suspicion. But this anti-malaria drug developed by the Army at taxpayer expense during the Vietnam War was subsequently marketed commercially by the pharmaceutical firms Hoffmann LaRoche and Smith Klein.

A long-simmering controversy about that anti-malaria drug prompted the Pentagon to abandon its own widespread use of mefloquine in 2013 because mefloquine HCL was found to cause permanent brain damage in rare cases. That action came only after the Food and Drug Administration warned sternly of neurologic side effects such as dizziness, loss of balance, ringing in the ears and possibly also anxiety, depression and hallucinations. Some of these effects can easily be mistaken for malingering, psychotic behavior or even the rash of what is now called post-traumatic stress disorder (PTSD).

Quinine

Quinine, the first modern answer to malaria, is a substance extracted from the bark of South America's chinchona tree. The Spanish learned about it in the 16th Century from the Inca. Quinine was isolated by French scientists in 1820 for use against fevers. German scientists synthesized it in 1934 in the form of chloroquine, the base of the popular class of anti-malaria drugs used ever since. After World War II chloroquine figured prominently in WHO's worldwide campaign to eradicate malaria. Hydroxychloroquine, a hot news topic since the outbreak of a new viral epidemic in 2019, is a less-toxic analog of chloroquine.

In Vietnam days we dutifully swallowed our medicine. Most veterans were grateful to Uncle Sam for protecting us from catching malaria. We had no idea what was in our black and yellow pills, and were blissfully unaware of any adverse consequences. But a few were less blissful to learn much later of medical findings that some of this stuff can also wreck your brain.

Coincidentally, in late 2019 someone sneezed in China and the whole planet was soon locked down by government edicts. And then, as the paralyzed Main Street economy of middle-class shops and small businesses was shuttered indefinitely while the Fed pumped trillions into bond and stock markets, a faint ray of hope shone down from frantic international medical practices.

Researchers in China, France and other foreign countries found that variants of the common anti-malaria drug, hydroxychloroquine, not only prevent the so-called COVID-19 virus but also are useful in treating virus patients. German chemical giant Bayer said chloroquine appears to have "broad-spectrum antiviral properties" and effects on immune response. Evidently, the mosquito-borne parasites targeted by the Pentagon's own laboratory since 1963 – and by the Army no later than the Panama Canal project – share a common Achilles' heel with the chimeric parasite causing the latest viral pandemic that vexed China, Iran and the rest of the world.

A prominent article dated 22 Aug. 2005 in *Virology Journal,* an official publication of the National Institutes of Health (NIH), had said: "Chloroquine is a potent inhibitor of SARS coronavirus infection and spread", treating it and its milder hydroxychloroquine as both a wonder drug and a vaccine. Even President Donald Trump confirmed at a March 2020 news conference that – presto! – the FDA was rapidly approving prescription of hydroxychloroquine to treat the mysterious corona virus (wherever it might actually have come from). He later revealed that he was also taking the drug as a prophylactic against the strange new virus that some experts says escaped from somebody's biological research laboratory. (Trump blamed the virus on China.)

In heuristic retrospect for Vietnam veterans, the U.S. Army's own black pill KO'ed the dreaded P. falciparum malaria parasite, whether or not it has any delayed consequences for the GI hosts. At least no veteran I know has complained of any brain-scrambling effects. Yet the government health bureaucracy, which actively supports private vaccine research, has now reversed itself regarding this inexpensive drug, discouraging its use for preventing or treating corona virus.

Agent Orange

Bad as it was, the surprise attack of the commie mosquitoes was quickly vanquished by a miraculous chemical compound. But another one of our own nifty synthetic chemicals caused us more vexing health problems. This was the blanket aerosol spraying of the forested war zones all around us with Agent Orange herbicide contaminated with deadly dioxin.

Heavy exposure to Agent Orange resulted in a mysterious skin malady later identified as chloracne. It was the bane of our black soldiers, some of whom suffered terribly. Several of my men came down with yellowish or dark cysts and painful pustules that disfigured their faces and sometimes spread to the torso and extremities.

Facial lumps and lesions made the army fetish of daily shaving impossible. The only foolproof remedy for this chloracne was to evacuate these men from the contaminated area. Whites were less affected by chloracne but no soldiers were immune to the dioxins permeating our unit's polluted environment. The Veterans Administration eventually linked Agent Orange exposure to a long list of cancers and other potentially fatal diseases for which thousands of veterans needed treatment. When my supply sergeant later sought VA care for a particularly aggressive and rare form of prostate cancer, our battalion commander filed an affidavit certifying that we were basically saturated with Agent Orange in War Zones C and D. The VA agreed – too late – that this was a service-related disease and paid.

I hope most of us got off easier. But Vietnam was left to cope with the persistent aftermath of chemical war on the environment, including congenital deformities, birth defects, dead forests, contaminated waterways and poisoned aquatic life.

–

Chapter 4

Night Attack

If the U.S. high command was actually surprised by the Tet offensive, it sure wasn't for lack of warnings. Even little Vietnamese children seemed to know that something really exciting was going to happen – like Boom, BOOM! And kids being kids, some discovered they could garner status points by trading on intriguing gossip they'd heard around their grownups.

I'm thinking here of a playful trio of boys, each no older than about eight years. From seemingly nowhere, they nonchalantly appeared among us one sultry day toward the end of November 1967 at the edge of the woods along Highway 13, which we had nicknamed Thunder Road. Amused by the unexpected company, a couple of bored riflemen shared with them some tropical chocolate bars from their C-rations.

A big northbound supply convoy was due to pass by any minute. It was on its way from Lai Khe, forward base of our First Infantry Division, to An Loc and Loc Ninh, the last garrisoned outposts before the Cambodian border. A cordon of security was needed to run this south-north gauntlet of about 90 kilometers. In our wooded sector, my infantry and armored personnel carriers lined the road for a couple of miles.

This being War Zone C, we were far from the nearest village. None of the usual motorbikes or Lambrettas with entrepreneurial mama-sans, papa-sans and working girls were cruising nearby, the road having been temporarily closed to civilian traffic. Munching their awful GI candy, the curious kids admired various items of army gear before approaching my dusty olive-drab M-113. It was easily identifiable as the command vehicle by two long whip antennae arching up and the number 306 stencelled in yellow on the side.

Our young guests seemed aware that they were in the presence of a *dai uy*, the captain in charge of this mechanized infantry company. Inscrutable Vietnamese was babbled when I asked where they had come from. Convinced that they were now just part of our team, one boy picked up a broken branch. He pointed it down at the laterite surface, ground to beige powder by the treads of many heavy armored vehicles. Capturing my attention, he began to draw conspiratorial symbols on the ground.

Could it be the location of buried land mines, the No. 1 nemesis of our tracked vehicles? Nope, guess again. The kid repeated his action a couple more times before I figured out that he was just tracing a single arabic numeral: 3. What could that mean? An omen? Our casual guests soon wandered off, leaving me to reflect. Briefly.

Asking for Trouble

A new artillery forward observer had joined us about ten days before. Like everyone else, he'd get his coveted combat infantry badge for logging just a month with us. But this hard-charging, red-haired first lieutenant wanted more. "Sir, I'm going to ask for a transfer to an outfit where something is happening," he confided on the ride back to our night defensive position. "It's too quiet for me here."

Ouch! That was embarassing. But true. Where on Earth were the local VC when we needed them? Our battalion hadn't seen serious action since October when the division had its hands full near the Michelin plantation to the west. So I talked up that outing like a lame excuse, hoping to string my eager comrade along with some fading glory. Both of us knew, of course, that a long lull in enemy activity is poison for a combat unit. Readiness, discipline and morale become casualties when the troops get bored. Worse, it can cause their leaders to make mistakes.

I wondered whether the lieutenant's rash wish for more excitement could coexist with my own strain of good luck. As a Swiss philosopher once put it: *Destiny has two ways to crush us – by refusing our wishes or by fulfilling them.* And the ironic gods know many ways to ground such flights of hubris. But I hoped this time they'd make allowances for some harmless machismo.

December got off to an equally uneventful start. We went walking in the woods for a change, a couple of dismounted platoons looking for Viet Cong, finding none. Someone heard a cock crow, the sign of a VC base camp somewhere in the vicinity. A tribe of monkeys made a racket in the treetops. All we found on the ground, though, was the corrugated sheet-iron roof of a long abandoned hooch that had once stood on a shallow depression.

Someone kicked aside the metal. This revealed a shiny jet-black scorpion, the largest I'd ever seen. From the robust twin pincer claws in front to the evil-looking stinger at the tip of the long, segmented tail, it could have passed for a young lobster. The luckless arachnid became our only body-count for the day.

We were sharing a fortified night defensive perimeter with a light infantry company of the 1st Battalion, 18th Infantry. My mech unit, Charlie Company, 2nd Battalion, 2nd Infantry, was temporarily on loan to the 1/18th, which had also put its command post here. The sun sets around 6:30 p.m. in the subtropical winter, twilight is brief and there was a daily ritual: curfew closes the road to civilians; company mess lines serve supper; on some days everyone mans his fighting position to test-fire weapon for one mad minute. Then the de-rigueur squad-sized ambush patrol leaves to take a position somewhere in the forest before nightfall.

My company's turn to furnish the patrol was the evening of 2 Dec. A squad from the First Platoon had the onus. A short burst of automatic fire greeted the departing file of eight camouflaged riflemen as they entered the woods about 150 yards west of Thunder Road. Stealth and surprise lost, the patrol leader followed standing orders: They returned. Now that we knew a hot reception awaited us out there, its mission was accomplished.

The gods thought otherwise. The brigade commander ordered another patrol dispatched, curtly dismissing our strong objections from the scene. This full colonel was micro-managing by radio from Lai Khe, 40 kilometers away. The capricious reversal of a trusted rule of engagement overshadowed morale like a partial eclipse. My men now knew that their company commander was not really in charge when it counted. The short straw then passed to my Second Platoon, the first having rightly protested that double jeopardy would be unfair – and against SOP.

Sgt. Blue's new night patrol saddled up quickly. He was a rugged and reliable man from a Midwestern farming region. But a compromise was made. His patrol could take an alibi position in a large pile of logs a few meters short of the treeline where contact had been made. This was a second mistake.

If a serious night attack is on the cards, a log pile is a lousy substitute for a well fortified encampment like our night defensive position (NDP). Our base was roughly a circle of about a hundred yards diameter. Grouped near the center were the battalion's headquarters tent, sandbag-ringed mortar firing points and parapets for mess crews and other support functions. The NDP's circumference was a ring of infantry fox holes with sleeping positions behind them, stiffened at regular intervals by my company's armored personnel carriers and a couple of light tanks on loan from the 4th Battalion, 64th Armor. Apart from the tanks' main guns, our armored vehicles each mounted a .50 caliber machine gun. We had about 20 of them. Each tracked vehicle was also dug in to a depth of at least a meter, the part of the hull still above ground protected on three sides with stacked sandbags. Our infantry sleeping positions were also partly dug in and protected above ground by sandbags that also made a mortar-proof double-layer roof supported by horizontal steel engineer stakes.

Foxholes in the First Infantry Division conformed to an elaborate defensive concept. Dubbed the Hays' hole after a former division commander, each had to be dug deep enough for two or three men to stand abreast with only their heads above ground level. The fighting hole was then capped by a flat sandbagged structure less than half a meter high, the firing ports protruding like big ears on the two outer corners. All of this was roofed with engineer stakes and sandbags that could withstand mortar impacts.

Each corner firing port formed a horizontal wedge, the narrow aperture at eye level inside the hole, the widening part flaring outward, diagonally across the front rather than directly toward an approaching enemy. This forced each rifleman or machine gunner to concentrate on a designated field of fire, crisscrossing that of the adjacent hole. Beyond the ports, straight lines of staked barbed wire extended outward from the interior angle of the wedge to snag attackers trying to avoid our saturating streams of lead. Since the firing ports did not look directly outward, the scheme emphasized continuous volumes of devastating, interlocking fires rather than precision marksmanship. Unlike the enemy, we packed tons of ammunition.

Each evening, small concave Claymore anti-personnel mines were also set out in front of the Hays' holes to be detonated at will by soldiers in the foxholes with electrical triggers connected by wires to the mines. Call it defense in depth. Beyond this lethal configuration was the first line of defense, concertina wire with razor-sharp barbs. Our NDP was surrounded by three concentric rings of extended concertina accordions, separated by corridors wide enough to drive our armored vehicles through. Each ring was a long pyramid of extended and staked concertina coils, one on top, two below it and three on the bottom. These three concentric pyramids of wire stood at least two meters high. Nothing was left to chance.

Thunder Road on our West side formed a north-south tangent to this fortified oval encampment. Except for a small sunken stream trickling past on the South side, the surrounding terrain was mostly flat. Army engineer Rome plows had cleared the forest for at least fifty meters on both sides of the road and all around our defensive perimeter. No movement in this empty zone went unobserved, at least in daylight. Lookouts with state-of-the-art Starlight night-vision scopes were posted dusk to dawn. There were cautionary tales of makeshift defensive positions being overrun elsewhere. but this one was practically impregnable to an attacking force lacking air support or proper artillery. The enemy was not yet convinced.

The weather was clear that evening. The overhead cargo hatch of my APC was left open to the starlight, the rear boarding ramp left down to benefit from the cool air. The night patrol had already reported zero activity around its position. I turned in for the night on the left fold-down bench of the APC, wrapping myself in a feather-light, camouflage-patterned poncho liner. My artillery FO occupied the right bench. Rank hath its privilege, in this case not having to bed down in the dirt outside.

Rude Awakening

About a half an hour after midnight, a deafening explosion ripped us out of deep sleep. It shook the 11-ton APC like an earthquake. The skin over my gut suddenly became a pin cushion for shrapnel. This surprise was instantly followed by a sustained staccato of blasts, one almost directly overhead. The acrid smell of cordite suffused the smoke-filled air. Struggling to retrieve my gear in the dark, I slid on something wet. The puddle on the metal track deck was the FO's blood. He was writhing on his bench, hands shielding his head. Still half naked, my first impulse upon this wicked awakening to December 3 was to get control of the chaos, somehow.

Paramedics swung into action. Our mess crew's sleeping parapet had taken a direct mortar hit. A couple of medics attended the wounded artillery lieutenant. Another bandaged my right shoulder as I tried to raise the patrol on the radio net. No response. The initial standoff attack with rockets, 82-mm mortars and accurate airbursts from rocket-propelled grenades (RPGs) had scored total surprise. The enemy seized the moment to move sappers into position on our wire barricades. Feigning an incursion from the North, his main assault massed on our western flank facing the road. But return fire from our foxholes soon started to pick up.

Machine guns and small arms took over the fight. Streams of tracers stitched through the blackness, theirs green or red, ours red only. Scattered muzzle flashes lit up the wood line along a 180-degree arc West to North. Their fearless sappers, toting wire cutting tools and bangalore torpedoes, were cut down before they could breach the outer circle of coiled barbed wire. The infantry assault that followed fared no better.

Artillery being mostly out of range, the battalion commander radioed for close air support. It arrived faster than expected. Out of the blackness came the ear-splitting shriek of the first jet fighter. Huge fireballs of red and white exploded just inside the western treeline. With amazing precision, the planes took turns making south-north napalm bombing runs. This spectacle drowned out the reports of small arms and machine guns. The shooting gradually became more sporadic.

Time to try retrieving the lost patrol? Conditions were less than propitious. My plan was to go out with a squad in defilade behind an APC. The NDP's own elaborate configuration now stood in the way. The vehicle portals in the three concentric walls of wire were offset from one another by a dozen yards. This forced the track driver to execute a slow slalom course back and forth, exposing the vehicle's flank to enemy RPG fire. The line of soldiers following it was left uncovered. To maneuver in the dark, we also needed to spotlight our movements with electric torches and vehicle headlights. No supporting fire could come from the defensive perimeter because we were in the way. Worse, once we reach the wood pile, it would be no easier getting back. Judging the mutiple risks to tip the scale, I called off this stunt in the middle. Another mistake?

In hindsight, yes. I should have pushed on. I should have groked that the heavy firepower from our NDP, their initial failure to breach it and the shock of the napalm runs had drained the fight out of the enemy. Such professional confidence would come only with experience that I was yet to gain. Nevertheless, the opening onslaught had left no one alive to rescue, with or without heroics.

The alibi position of night patrol had been directly in the path of the enemy's concentrated assault on the NDP's front entrance. Not even a miracle could have saved it from being overrun and wiped out in the first minutes. That's just what had happened. The stiffening bodies of seven men were recovered at first light. Shot through the heart, the eighth GI killed in this action was a seasoned master sergeant with our sister light infantry company. He was nearing the end of his third tour in the same war, one too many.

Helicopters evacuated 21 wounded men from my company, including the mess crew. My gung-ho FO was a casualty. Without an eye, his budding career in the field artillery was over. The sister unit probably dusted off half a dozen the morning of 3 December. I thought again of that cryptic numeral the local boy had repeatedly traced in the dust. Maybe he expected our days were numbered, but his prophetic warning sure didn't come out of any bible.

Like the U.S. Army, both VC and NVA go to extremes to take their dead and wounded with them. A daylight sweep of the area counted about five enemy bodies. These were NVA regulars. A sapper's pink, disembodied brain was found like an anatomy specimen tangled in our barbed wire a meter above his abandoned bangalore torpedo. Wrapped in a poncho a couple of hundred meters away was one of the slain NVA soldiers. A strapping young Northerner, at least as tall as I am, he would have towered over villagers here in Cochin, where local VC were typically petit. Naturally, official reports of the encounter later featured a somewhat exaggerated body count.

Daily operations orders had included not just the boilerplate intelligence reference to the legendary Ninth VC Regiment but also unit designations 271 and 272 for a couple of NVA regiments supposedly in our area. Since current locations and movements of these elusive formations were apparently unknown, the information had been fairly useless to us, thus easily ignored.

What we encountered was determined to have been a reinforced NVA battalion. If so, the enemy commander would have been overconfident. A rule of thumb calls for an adequate attacking force to outnumber the defenders of a strong point by a factor of three. Our fortified NDP may have contained almost three hundred well armed soldiers. The only fly in the ointment was the location of my night patrol, which partly inhibited effective fire against the assaulting force.

Nevertheless, this night attack had been carefully planned and thoroughly rehearsed. And the defeat did not deter the NVA from trying again. Separate assaults with stronger forces were launched against two more NDPs further north on Thunder Road in the next couple of weeks. The results were the same, a tribute to the sensible defensive doctrine of the Big Red One. VC units already knew that trying to take one of our field bases was fool's errand. But the NVA probably regarded these operations as good practice for their impending Lunar New Year offensive against the sprawling support bases ringing Saigon. That main act called Tet commenced on 31 January 1968.

—

Chapter 5

Lai Khe Fireworks

Give the troops a break! That's what the Big Red One intended with the morale-boosting policy of letting its combat units in the field stand down roughly once a month in Lai Khe. These rotating mini-vacations lasted only three days. But there was plenty of beer in the rear and a bevy of cute young Vietnamese masseuses waiting nearby at the famous Lai Khe steambaths.

The heavily loaded armored personnel carriers of Charlie Company rumbled single-file through the North Gate on schedule 20 December 1967. Men of our rear detachment greeted them with huge brimming barrels, ordered by our First Sergeant. They tossed cans of ice-cold Miller's, Pabst's and Budweiser up to each of the thirsty soldiers atop the passing tracks. It was party time.

In the planet-girdling archipelago of U.S. Army bases, Lai Khe may have been the most attractive and possibly the greenest of all. It had been a French experimental rubber plantation. A couple of handsome colonial buildings had been repurposed as brigade headquarters, staff offices and a medical clinic. There was also an officers' club with transient billets and comfortable quarters for senior officers and a few civilians, such as the Red Cross special services girls known as "doughnut dollies". Each resident unit also had its own cluster of wooden barracks with a recreation room. The ever popular steambaths made the leafy base seem almost like a spa.

East met West in Lai Khe. Laundry, haircuts, stationery and trinket vending, nursing assistance, even bar tending were the province of Vietnamese civilians. They lived in a fenced-off hamlet that was entirely surrounded by the big military base athwart Highway 13 about 40 miles north of Saigon. On special occasions the mama-san manager of the steambaths would even deign to treat a few favored captains to her delicious Vietnamese cooking. Lai Khe's local Vietnamese staff knew the base inside out and were undoubtedly privvy to some of its lesser military secrets.

The Lai Khe military installation was roughly an elipse of about three miles long and a mile wide. An improved, widened stretch of the highway served as a north-south airstrip for helicopters and light planes. It sliced through the middle of the base, civilian road traffic having been diverted around the eastern flank outside the fortified perimeter. Apache country was on the west.

Thanks to the rubber trees and an abundance of undisturbed greenery, there were secluded niches within Lai Khe. One of them was Snuffy's bar and grill, where fine whiskey flowed and the cuisine probably deserved a Michelin star. Prime quality steaks, rumored to have migrated from the general's mess, were Snuffy's specialty. Army Jeeps with familiar unit markings waited, parked outside on special evenings while fortunate officers with invitations dined within.

The best of these commanders' jeeps, incidently, could become hot items at Lai Khe. They tended to vanish suddenly and then reappear with the markings of a different unit. That was, at least, what Bravo Six's thought had happened to his own missing vehicle. He later mentioned that my new company jeep looked suspiciously familiar. I promised to investigate.

Supply sergeants are notoriously resourceful in their efforts to replace essential items of equipment like AN-PRC-25 radios that won't work properly. Requisitioning through normal supply channels takes days but bona fide combat losses were swiftly replaced. Perhaps that why so many defective radios tended to return from the field with fresh bullet holes always blamed on the VC.

I got a practical lesson in colonial customs at the Chinese family laundry that served our company barracks. Hoping to chat up the very cute teenaged daughter who was usually behind the counter, I picked up my wash in person. On duty this time was her father. He instantly recognized the company *dai uy* and politely declined to accept my cash, a perquisite that apparently went with my status as the current patron of his enterprise.

The Big Bang

At high noon on Day Three of our Lai Khe stand-down, Charlie Company was standing at attention in ranks in front of our barracks' mess hall. Our battalion commander, LTC Henry L. Davisson, had called an inspection. It was not to be. As Daring Six returned my salute, a stupendous detonation shook the earth.

That was just the dramatic overture. Pulsing decibel levels then defiantly tested lower and higher octaves – from a mad din like midnight on New Year's Eve to the blasting stacatto of a passing truck that suddenly lost its muffler. Since the sustained auditory assault was coming from the westerly direction of the base's munitions storage depot, we knew instantly what was happening. These were the tonal reports of fresh ammuntion magazines cooking off in chaotic sequence.

As the Big Red One's forward base, much of the division's munition stockpile was held in Lai Khe's arsenal. Even a tone-deaf ear could pick out the shifting sources of the explosive concert: 8-inch, 155-mm, 175-mm, 105-mm artillery projectiles and their propellent charges; 4-inch and 81-mm mortar rounds and propellent charges: 90-mm recoilless rifle and light tank munitions, helicopter gunship rockets; .50- and .30- caliber machine gun belts; 7.62-mm rifle bullets; claymore mines, hand grenades, thump-gun grenades, pyrotechniques, .45 caliber bullets for tommy guns and sidearms, and more. At military contracting prices, this spectacular bonfire alone may well have jacked up the national debt.

Wanton destruction was the visible effect but the cause remained only a guess. Rumor had it that the VC left note calling it retaliation for a recent nearby fire fight. Informed stateside news stories subsequently speculated on infiltrating VC sappers with satchel charges or pinned the blame on a direct hit of a 122-mm VC heavy rocket on an artillery magazine. Whatever the cause, the ensuing sound and light show continued for at least the next 12 hours.

The long row of exploding ammo magazines stretched along the southwestern part of the base between the central airstrip and the fortified western perimeter of Lai Khe. The outer defensive barrier of earthen berms and barbed wire fencing was backed up by a string of pill boxes, bunkers and observation towers. Guards manning these fortified positions were trapped in place by the sporadic barrages of jagged steel from the ordnance popping behind them. They needed to be relieved and replaced by a fresh shift.

Within an hour my battalion commander told me to join him near the center of Lai Khe just east of the airstrip, the brigade headquarters being too close to lethal cascades of flying detrius from the exploding magazines. There we met with our distraught brigade commander to coordinate a defense of the base. Counting jeep drivers there were six of us at this impromptu tactical parley under the rubber trees.

The relentless weight of command responsibility exacts a toll on any officer's nerves. But hardly anything could be more humiliating than losing his command's munition stocks to anonymous guerrillas in black pajamas and flip-flops. Few human anxieties top that of a possible blot on the promising career trajectory of a highly ambitious line officer. The brigade commander, pondering his base layout diagram, collapsed in tears on the hood of his jeep. At that moment the 2/2's Daring Six took command of the defense of Lai Khe.

His first order was to retrieve the trapped guards on the western perimeter. Charlie Company's platoons were assigned sectors and my men mounted their tracks. We ran the APCs, soldiers safe inside for a change, through the hail of steel pelting the many bunkers from behind. Our men took over the defensive positions as the relieved guards left in our buttoned-down APCs. This worked without a hitch.

There was no getting past the popping depot without an armored vehicle. My evening command post was a jeep with a couple of ANPRC-25 radios. As we monitored the changing of the guard, another magazine blew sky high. My driver/RTO and I scurried for cover under the jeep, where we chatted until the inferno moved on to the next magazine. Tic-tac-toe played in the sand by moonlight killed some time between showers of shrapnel.

With the perimeter guard rotation restored, fires and detonations subsided, leaving an eerie quiet by first light. Our new mission was to assist a team from Explosive Ordnance Disposal (EOD). Their job was to collect the unexploded artillery projectiles scattered in all directions around the ruined depot. That required lots of extra manpower and the uncommon nerve for which the Army's EOD men were deservedly famous. Learning by example, we wary infantrymen were soon tossing heavy 8-inch rounds like jumbo jelly beans onto the steel beds of five-ton trucks. It turned out to be good training for a later operation. We then gladly returned to the field, where tight night defensive perimeters make tougher targets for VC stand-off attacks.

The ammo dump debacle probably raised the readiness curve at Lai Khe. But a stealthy nighttime sapper infiltration soon afterward reduced the officers' club and its second-floor transient billets to a pile of smoking rubble. A veteran chopper pilot and a newly arrived lieutenant colonel crawled out of the debris almost intact, except for frazzled nerves.

Air Mail

Charlie Company had a scarier rendezvous with heavy unexploded ordinance in March. Intelligence had somehow learned of a few dozen unexploded 8-inch artillery rounds lying around in a woods on the eastern fringe of the Iron Triangle about 10 miles south of Lai Khe. We were dispatched to destroy this ammunition before the enemy could scoop out the encased explosive material to recycle against us as land mines, claymores or booby-traps.

The rounds had been deliberately fired by an allied ARVN artillery battery as an aerial delivery of fresh munitions to appreciative kin in the VC, explained Daring Six. We found these gift projectiles, still safely nose-capped with their steel shipping plugs, scattered all across a quarter-acre field. Our job was to rig them by hand for demolition with C4 charges and detonating cord.

This was a ticklish task for mere infantry, since the heavy projectiles could have been armed or at least sensitized from flying for miles after being blasted out of some distant artillery pieces. Worse, they could also have been booby-trapped after landing. If disturbed, just one of them would leave a truck-sized crater if it went off. And that detonation might touch off the others, we feared. We did our rigging with extreme care before backing off a couple of hundred yards from ground zero. At that crucial point we were suddenly ordered to leave. Perhaps the command had decided it was more prudent to let the EOD experts blow up the woods.

In the first month of Tet, the brigade base started to experience daily mortar and rocket attacks. One hundred and thirty attacks were tallied in February alone. The sporadic bombardments never lasted long enough to be localized so that we could respond with artillery. But they were cunningly timed to disrupt the mess hall meal schedules or to roust resident units out of their barracks bunks and into the dug-in shelters at odd hours of the night. Called back to the defense of Lai Khe in March, Charlie Company's soldiers spent some sleepless wee hours in our mortar-proof, sand-bagged connex containers, listening to incoming ordnance impacting nearby. The safest place on the base seemed to be the Vietnamese hamlet in the middle.

One such shelling demonstrated the pinpoint accuracy the VC could achieve with rockets usually launched from flimsy bamboo tripods erected in the woods. By that time, late spring, I had joined the brigade staff and a few of us were taking a soda break in a makeshift wooden building with a corrugated sheet-iron roof. I and another captain, an academy classmate, hit the ground simultaneously, nose to nose behind a flimsy quarter-inch plywood partition – a reaction so ridiculously futile that we shared a good laugh at ourselves.

When it was safe to look outside, it became clear that rockets had targeted more than the brigade commander's mansion. A column of brown smoke about ten yards away was also rising from the colonel's pride – a huge, newly delivered, custom-built, mobile command post, both motorized and armored, with a cute turret on top. It took a direct hit. Some VC rocketeer must have won a medal for that precision.

–

Chapter 6

The French Fort

An old French fort about 15 miles north of Lai Khe served as one of the few reliable landmarks in the otherwise featureless terrain along Highway 13. This former strongpoint on the west side of Thunder Road was now just a sagging hill of earth and rocks poking hardly three meters above the remains of a narrow-gauge railroad that had once served local rubber plantations.

Most of the steel rails had likely been scavanged and sold to Saigon's scrap metal dealers long ago. But a few dozen meters of useless rusting track still paralleled the north-south road below the triangular fort. One section of tracks looped defiantly skyward like a carnival roller-coaster. The rest lay bent, curved or severed on the ground like dead serpents. Behind the fort to the West were acres of tall elephant grass with a big forest beyond that.

Our mechanized unit often passed this place on search-and-destroy missions. On the map it was marked Ap Bau Bang, a hamlet long abandoned. Maybe the villagers had joined the Viet Cong who were quite active in the surrounding forests. We never bothered to inspect the crumbling ruins. Except as a mile marker, the little fort was too small and exposed to interest either us or the VC.

A few miles up the road to the North, next to the village of Chon Thanh, was a big artillery fire base protected by infantry units that came and went. A couple of self-propelled artillery batteries, 8-inch and 155-mm, were in residence. Every night the big guns shot harrassing and interdicting (H&I) fires into the surrounding free-fire zone. This was War Zone C, where our ordnance was free to make craters helter-skelter. Whoever might be living in the woods was considered hostile.

In late January 1968 Charlie Company was loaned temporarily to the infantry battalion currently securing this artillery fire base, where light sleepers definitely needed ear plugs. The constant commotion in fire base Caisson IV should have kept local wildlife at bay. But U.S. bases contain food and even GI cuisine attracts rats. In Vietnam, the presence of well-fed rats is irrestisible for hungry cobras, making them welcome guests in rural villages like Chon Thanh. Their job is rat control. The snakes hunt the rats in the litter under the floors of the houses, which are usually raised about half a meter above the ground.

One evening before the H&I fires commenced a few of us observed a huge black cobra on silent patrol in and out of our barbed wire barrier. A serpent of this length could have spit in a soldier's eye if annoyed. I reckoned it could also have reared its flared snout right up to the top of an APC.

The leg battalion commander came up with an idea that was worse than the noise of the guns. He wanted to parcel out my APCs piecemeal on S&D missions with his infantry. Requisitioned as needed, my tracks, with or without their squads, would then operate under the control of his platoon leaders or company commanders. I objected strongly that the integrity of my unit would be lost. My platoon leaders and I would then be relegated to playing poker or reading dime novels in the fire base, while our men and equipment were out beating the bush with somebody else's unit.

My own battalion commander interceded for us with his peer. But the issue vanished by itself when that infantry battalion was replaced by another in the fire base. The new unit was the 1st Battalion, 16th Infantry, commanded by Lieutenant Colonel Calvert Benedict. A tall, slender, bald-headed officer, his serious demeanor somehow recalled that farmer depicted in the painting *American Gothic*. The 1/16th had been bloodied in a couple of large engagements the previous autumn during the corp's Shenandoah II campaign near the Michelin plantation. Benedict had earned a reputation for fearlessness under fire.

Toward midnight on 28 January, a day or two after the 1/16th arrived, one of their night patrols sprang its ambush. A lively fire fight ensued and the patrol radioed for backup.* It was ensconced in the French fort, too far away for timely reinforcement with leg infantry but perfect for my mech company. We saddled up two platoons in a couple of minutes. The battalion commander decided to ride along on my command track. He told me he was curious to see how mounted infantry operated but that the rest was my show.

48

As my nine tracks raced southward on Highway 13, I radioed the plan to the platoon leaders. When our mech column came abreast of the fort, the lead platoon would pass it while the second platoon and my track would stop on the near side. Then we would all immediately pivot, driving to the west on both flanks of the fort before opening fire with .50's and dismounting our infantry squads.

We were greeted by rifle fire from the elephant grass. Some VC maneuvered toward us, maybe hoping to infiltrate between our tracks or pick off any men still on top. A confused shooting match erupted at nearly point-blank range right in front of the line of APCs. Darkness made it hard to tell friend from foe just by muzzle flashes. It was one of the very few times my .45-caliber sidearm came in handy. Benedict loped over to his own men still firing down from a recess on the flat top of the fort.

A nighttime action creates an attractive visual effect. In heavy use the barrels of .50 caliber machine guns begin to glow cherry red. Unless a hot barrel is changed with an asbestos glove, another round could cook off or the gun could "run away" by feeding itself. The gunner or his assistant would then have to break the self-feeding ammunition belt with a violent twist. When these guns quit firing, the barrels must be elevated to make sure no one is inadvertently shot off the next track. A wooden block can be put in the receiver for good measure.

When the gunplay stopped, we retrieved a couple of wounded VC prisoners from the nearby brush. A better look at the ambush scene would have to wait until daylight. One POW was laid out on my track's bench. The vehicle was full of ammunition, including hand grenades. The prisoner made a sudden movement as if to sit up. Impulsively, I smacked his head down on the taut canvass. One of my soldiers said, Wow! I detailed him to guard the prisoner and the ammo on the ride back.

Cool Cal

Soon afterward, Charlie Company left the artillery base for other business. The next time I saw Benedict was months later in Lai Khe. I had accepted an invitation to a formal brigade officers' dinner in a colonial mansion that must have belonged to the former French plantation manager. He was seated diagonally across from me at the long table, linen-covered and set for about 25 guests, who mostly outranked me. The food was several grades above mess-line fare. Servants in white smocks scuttled back and forth, refilling wine, whiskey and Cognac glasses. Army brass had relaxed comfortably into old colonial customs. I wondered whether we'd be treated to cigars, preferably Havana, before the evening ended. Naturally, the conversation was mostly military shop talk.

The VC must have read the invitation. They broke up the party with a rocket attack. The first couple of rounds impacted convincingly, right in front of the mansion. Dinner guests sprinted for the sand-bagged underground bunker located directly outside a rear entrance to the dining hall. I was about to join them when I noticed that one aloof figure was in no such hurry. It was mesmerizing to watch Benedict casually wipe his lips with the linen napkin while rising nonchalantly to join the herd. His serene composure never changed.

This officer was already something of a legend in the ranks. Lt. Don Stuckey, who led my 2nd Platoon, had come to us from the 1/16th when that battalion was brought back up to strength after a series of major engagements. He shared recollections of that fighting near the Michelin during Shenandoah II. It sounded like his old unit had the knack of attracting enemies like a porch light draws swarms of moths.

A classmate of mine commanded one of Benedict's units. Three days before the Ong Thanh ambush of the 2/28th, his rifle company disembarked from helicopters at an NVA base camp defended by a stay-behind force. The next several hours they were engaged in what he remembered as "the heaviest fight … during my tour." His 1/16th company lost five men that day. In early January he said his company also swept an enemy-occupied village just south of Lai Khe, decimating an enemy force in his last action before rotating to division staff.

Another oft-told anecdote about Benedict in particular made the rounds in the division. A patrol posted outside the defensive wire had been chewed up when his battalion turned back an NVA attack on its night defensive position. Most of this patrol managed to get back inside but a relief force had to be sent after a couple of wounded men. Enemy fire stymied the rescue attempt. To their amazement, the battalion commander took the lead, not in a low crawl but walking upright. Reaching the wounded soldiers, he personally carried one of them back to the perimeter. This display of sangfroid caused those who witnessed it to wonder whether their leader was bullet-proof.

Decades later the name of this stoical officer came up in an e-mail exchange between me and Bravo Six, reminiscing about our time together in the 2/2 Infantry. Like me, Bravo Six always braced for unpleasant times when our mech companies were loaned out to leg infantry battalions for this or that operation. But he also shared my respect for Benedict. Neither one of us could complain of any unfairness when working for his 1/16th Infantry battalion. Benedict never asked anyone to do what he wouldn't do himself. That ethic set him apart from lesser men.

—

* This 28-29 Jan. action was described in the division's General Order Number 3070 of 4 April 1968, which said five enemy combatants were killed and two taken prisoner. Benedict, West Point class of 1945, retired with two stars after having commanded the Berlin Brigade in the occupied enclave of Germany before the fall of the wall in the 1980s.

Chapter 7

Friendly Fire

TET began with a wake-up call for Charlie Company. Still yawning, scratching and stretching, my men were barely out of their sand-bagged sleeping positions when rockets and mortar rounds impacted helter-skelter inside our night defensive position. Breakfast had to wait.

This was the start of February 1968, a day etched in memory. The rude reveille aside, it was the only time in my life I was ever astonished to gaze at a perfectly clear sky of the wrong color. The sky was bright green. But quirky meteorology was not my immediate concern this morning.

Surprising as it was, the VC standoff attack was pretty brief. There was no followup on the ground and apparently no one inside our wire had been hurt. Reckoning that the impudent ordnance must have arched across Highway 13, a/k/a Thunder Road, from someplace in the brush about two hundred meters east of our perimeter, my 81-mm mortars responded with their own barrage. With our listening posts pulled in, a squad was dispatched into the brush across the road to locate the source of the dawn intrusion.

They had no trouble finding it. Unlike VC rockets, the heaviest of which, 122-mm, can sound like a freight train barreling through the sky, mortars are pretty sneaky, high-trajectory weapons. They can be set up quickly just about anywhere and usually only radar can locate the source of an incoming barrage. The VC use an 82-mm version that could conveniently also fire equivalent U.S. mortar ammunition in a pinch. But the base plates of these tubes need a small, relatively level firing point. So do the light VC rockets that also require a portable bamboo tripod for launching. Our squad soon recovered a few artifacts, including the aiming device the VC left behind.

It made an unusual trophy for our battalion. This sighting instrument was ingeniously hand-carved out of balsa and bamboo with makeshift glass lenses glued into a wooden cylinder. The VC were gone but the prints and trampled vegetation revealed how their primitive artillery was quietly deployed during the night.

Charlie Company had its "Thunder" NDP all to itself. One of our jobs that day was to guard the Rome plow bulldozers of an engineer unit. These tracked behemoths were busy cutting back the forest on the western side of the road about half a mile south of our Thunder encampment. One of my infantry platoons was sent out there to protect them.

This platoon came under fire from the woods at mid-morning. They reported casualties. The operator of an engineer bulldozer had both forearms amputated by a rocket-propelled grenade (RPG). A medic was attending to one of our men when I arrived. The dying soldier had a hideous chest wound from an RPG. We watched as shock turned the man's sallow complexion to a shade of gray. My frustrated medic scooped up his gear and moved on to the next wounded soldier.

The foreboding color of the daytime sky over this field of felled trees and damaged men became the astral phenomenon I associate most with Vietnam's Lunar New Year. It so happened that the two infantrymen killed this first day of Tet had previously made for bad blood among the local people. Both were pending court martial for the rape of the young wife of a prominent village chief. They were accused of stopping a bus during one of our convoy security details and abducting the prettiest girl among the passengers. If true, the Army's case had just been closed by a higher authority.

Charlie Company and the rest of our battalion rarely occupied the same position for more than a couple of days during Tet. We moved all around the two war zones. In War Zone D east and southeast of Lai Khe, the south-flowing river Song Be joins the larger Song Dong Nai. Several looping meanders in a cup-like river bend had carved a geography known to us as the Catcher's Mitt. Fat fingers of dry land between the riverine meanders were aptly nicknamed The Testicles. Charlie Company and Bravo Company established separate NDPs along a dirt track a couple of miles west of those fingers targeted for our mounted search & destroy missions.

Bravo's NDP was about four miles south of ours. The rest of the battalion camped still further south. A rice farming area speckled with some small hamlets began a few miles west of us, making our north-south string of encampments an obstacle to enemy units trekking between the river crossings and villages.

Our operation order for the first day in our new position was to enter the Catcher's Mitt configuration on an easterly heading from a specific point on the dirt road at an appointed time, EDT. To do that our column first had to move south a couple of miles roughly parallel to the road and then pivot east toward the winding river, where we might trap some hostile force in one of the testicles. Between the road and the river were rows of rubber trees and good visibility. To avoid alerting the enemy to our true intentions, I chose to approach our starting checkpoint through the dense woods and jungle just west of the road.

Such was the plan. Its execution was more interesting. We had progressed at least a mile when we drew frontal small arms fire from the south. I spread our formation and began closing on the enemy. The firing gained intensity. Some light machine guns began their chatter from the woods in front of us. I radioed my NDP's mortars with target coordinates for a fire mission. Daring Six came up on the battalion net, ordering an immediate check-fire of my mortars, an action that puzzled me.

The gunfire, ours and theirs, intensified. Somewhere overhead droned Daring Six's H-13 helicopter. He was soon joined by a bigger chopper, a C&C Huey. We also started to hear the sound of heavy machine guns. Bravo Company's mission and movements were unknown to me. Daring Six suddenly came up again on the battalion net to check-fire our sister company's .50 calibers. By this time we already had one wounded soldier. Given the volume of fire, we could have expected many more. But we were told to halt our advance because the assistant division commander circling overhead had been promised a quick airstrike. The jets dropped their ordnance on a deep overgrown gully that intersected the dirt road about two hundred yards in front of us.

The shooting abated, then all but stopped. Charlie Company moved ahead to check out the V-shaped gully, which deepened and widened in the westerly direction. There we spotted elements of Bravo halted high on south side. Daring Six's H-13 landed on the road nearby. He called for me and Bravo Six to come meet him – with our maps.

Our boss calmly grilled us, one after the other, on why we were at this location at this time, how we got here and what we understood our instructions to have been. After a mutual time hack, he sent us back to scour the gully and the surrounding woods and brush for enemy soldiers, dead or alive. Our body count for the day was lying at the bottom of the gully. It was a cow, freshly riddled with hunks of Air Force shrapnel.

The after-action report recounted how a small VC patrol moving through the gully made its escape toward the west. Before leaving, this patrol must have dispatched small teams to fire almost simultaneously at both our mech companies approaching from the North and the South, enticing each to close on an elusive enemy in the middle.

That's not implausible. I later learned that VC units took great pains to learn our radio frequencies and unit call-signs. With informants everywhere, they were also keen observers, collected tactical information on our locations and movements, were well aware of our standard procedures and anticipated our typical reactions. Yet there may have been a simpler scenario. Whatever happened, Charlie Company never did lay eyes on the river or its testicles that day. And for some reason the great Catcher's Mitt firefight never afterward became a topic of open discussion among our battalion's commanding officers.

Untimely Departures

My favorite editorial cartoon of the Vietnam War showed two dusty GIs taking cover in a foxhole as assorted incoming ordnance exploded all around them and a bullet nipped off half the cigarette one had just lit up. This soldier remarks to his buddy: Going by the volume of incoming fire, I'd say that's either a reinforced NVA heavy weapons platoon or it's Bravo Company.

I had spotted that gem in a March 1968 edition of *Stars & Stripes*, a week or two after my friend, Bravo Six, had been dusted off in another Tet firefight, this time near Bau Bang in War Zone C. He was shot the day before he was slated to vacate his command for a coveted staff position as assistant brigade operations office in Lai Khe. And he wasn't the only one whom luck then deserted.

Within a week of that action, the commander of Alpha Company, Capt. Wilford Carey, was similarly shot up. Also medically mustered out of the Army, Alpha Six found a new career as a judge in Oregon. Both 2/2 company commanders were treated in the same military hospitals on their way home. Their untimely departures left me more nervous than was usual.

I included the *Stars & Stripes* cartoon clipping in a "get-well-soon" note to Bravo Six, still somewhere in the Army's emergency medical circuit before he and Alpha Six were flown out of Vietnam. Crippling multiple gunshot wounds to the hip and leg ended a very auspicious military career for Capt. George "Sonny" Gratzer. He earned two Silver Stars during his tour.

We stayed penpals until his death about five year ago. A good Vietnam war novel* and three volumes of poetry he later wrote back home in Montana are on my bookshelf. "Ed, Im glad we had these experiences together – or at least in the same organization. We even shot at each other a couple of times", he confided in a 2002 letter. "What the hell, it was thrilling and I'll never forget all of it, although, as I said before, I wish I could remember *all* of it."

Roger that, Sonny. Me too.

–

* *Ninety Days* by Sonny Gratzer (iUniverse, Inc. Bloomington, Indiana 2013)

Chapter 8

Bad Bees, Good Turtles

The morning of 4 February 1968 found Charlie Company pulling road security on Highway 13 in Binh Duong province a few miles north of Lai Khe. Another supply convoy was due to make the run up Thunder Road. It looked like our mounted gang of deputy traffic cops might be blessed with an uneventful day. Tranquility was running rampant in our little sector.

Eight or ten miles due east of us was the town of Phuoc Vinh, base of the First Brigade of the First Infantry Division and an ARVN garrison. Between them and us was a broad expanse of flat, wooded terrain through which the Song Be river flowed down from the north. Beyond Phuoc Vinh was just more forest stretching eastward another dozen miles to the foot of the highlands.

We knew the area both east and west of our sector on Highway 13 from many a search & destroy mission. This particular place on the map was called Bau Bang, a village now ruined and abandoned. A secondary route numbered 301 branched southeast from here in the direction of the Song Be. It led past another abandoned hamlet, Ap Bo La, to a crossing point on the river. We preferred to avoid 301, knowing from sad experiences that it was usually mined.

Running along the east side of Highway 13, a/k/a Thunder Road, was an intermittent stream in a deep gully. This was an insurmountable barrier to our tracked vehicles. The only access to secondary road 301 was to cross the gully on a narrow "bridge", supported by a concrete culvert, less than a hundred yards east of Highway 13. This bridge was just a raised section of the laterite side road. But trying to enter that road this way was not the brightest idea unless this chokepoint could first be cleared by foot soldiers with mine sweepers. On this day of road security duty, we had no reason to bother with that.

Charlie Company's peace was shattered in mid-afternoon by an urgent radio call from Daring Six. A light infantry company from the First Brigade was heavily engaged with a much larger NVA unit about three miles southeast of us on Route 301. They were in serious trouble and we were to ride immediately to their relief.*

Mech to the Rescue

I collected my platoons in open woods just west of Thunder Road, told them the situation and gave them an order of march. Time to depart, but my lead platoon wasn't moving. The lieutenant in charge radioed back something about his men's concerns over the unswept chokepoint. Bau Bang, distinguished here by some rusting wreckage of an ill-fated fuel-tanker truck, was aptly named. The nearby stream culvert, nicknamed Claymore Corners, was the dreaded intersection of 301 with Thunder Road.

Unforgotten by my troops was what had happened to Bravo's command track here on 14 September. Fresher in memory were several more of Charlie's and Bravo's anti-tank mine encounters along the jinxed side road. Soldiers train to return hostile gunfire, but there is no answer to a hidden charge that can flip a squad's armored personnel carrier like an airborne flapjack. All eyes were now fixed anxiously on the gully crossing awaiting us to the East.

With a bit theatrical cussin' for effect, I changed the platoons' order of march and gave a second order to move out. Radio silence. Not one peep. Despite my George Patton imitation, no track budged from the spot. This was major trouble. It instantly called for Plan B.

So, let's do it this way, I told the leaders. You and your drivers will cover down on the tread marks left by the first APC that gets across onto 301. All three Roger-ed in turn. Switching to vehicle intercom I told Sp4 Guadeloupe, my veteran command track driver, to move us up to the head of our column. We would take the dare.

I have a natural aversion to theatrics. I suspect that even our famous two-word Infantry motto was shouted more often by Hollywood actors in war movies than by real riflemen in actual combat. But this impasse was beyond melodrama. It was our moment of truth. When all platoon leaders were back on the net, I gave the classic order: "Follow me!"

58

On cue, Guadeloupe revved the command track's engine to a high-pitched scream. APC #306 charged forward, churning up a dust cloud. We barrelled over the unswept chokepoint near top speed with twelve dozen skeptical pairs of eyes waiting to see whether we'd reach the other side in one piece. None was more surprised than me and my crew. Charlie Company's three mounted platoons immediately rumbled after us onto Route 301. That was half the battle. Our mission began to feel exhilarating. We quickened the pace of our column of 14 tracks.

Rome plows had long since made low tangles of deadfall out of the woods about a dozen yards on either side of the road. My command track found a place near the middle of the column. The leaders were told to guide their vehicles if possible on the tread marks of those ahead. Gunners herring-boned their .50 caliber machine guns left and right, ready to rake any ambush from either side of the road.

Nearing the place where the light infantry company was supposed to be, I noticed my soldiers atop the tracks ahead of me firing their M16s and M79s at the woods on our right. They were returning sniper fire I had barely heard. Like all the leaders and track drivers, I wore a CVC helmet on the march. This communications helmet has a microphone, a switch to change radio frequencies and built-in speakers covering both ears.

Hostile small arms fire increased on the next stretch of road. Concealed in the brush to our left was that ghost hamlet, Ap Bo La. I had the first two platoons pivot their eight tracks to the right. Their squads dismounted and advanced in a skirmish line toward the forest where the enemy seemed to be concentrated. Halfway from the road to the wood line, our track gunners opened up with their heavy machine guns. Ignoring the fire from the woodline, my gunner struggled to clear our .50 caliber, which had suddenly jammed in the middle of the shootout. Meanwhile, the third platoon spread out behind us as a reserve on the opposite side of the road. Their main job was to make sure we couldn't be surprised from the rear.

There was something wrong here. We were gradually suppressing the AK-47 and automatic-rifle fire, but the hostiles in the woods hadn't used heavy machine guns or the B-40/RPGs, their best anti-armor weapon. Could this be a diversion? The only way to find out was to maneuver some infantry squads into the woods where isolated APCs would be sitting ducks. But we still didn't know the whereabouts of the light infantry company we were sent to extract. Daring Six had the answers.

His H-13 helicopter appeared overhead. He had made radio contact with the beleaguered leg company. My platoons on line should hold fast, he said. He directed me to follow the lead of his low-flying chopper with half of the reserve platoon. Leaving the road behind our right flank, we headed northeast through the bush for about three hundred yards. Here the chopper turned sharply to the right. We followed in column down a treacherously narrow path that may once have been a paddy dike. It was hemmed in by tall, dense bushes on both sides. These green walls restricted visibility to little more than an arm's length.

As I took a status report from a platoon leader, something odd distracted me. We must have knocked down a hive. Angry bees too fast to swat were now buzzing around my perch atop the moving command track. The CVC helmet muted their sounds to vague swishing, hissing and zissshing. In their wake I watched twigs and leaves snap off cleanly in front of my nose. Bees don't do that. This was heavy sniper fire coming from multiple unseen sources in the dense thickets on either side of the overgrown path. We lacked clear targets and room to maneuver. So we stepped up the pace.

A hundred yards onward came a quieter stretch with better visibility. Just beyond the trees and bushes on the right of our little column was a large pond. The partly shaded expanse of opaque blue-gray water was pock marked with darker round shapes I took to be big swamp turtles. As we moved into view, a few of these olive-green carapaces began to stir. A couple of them levitated slowly above the water's surface. These turtle shells were the camouflaged helmets of submerged infantrymen. We had finally found at least part of the light infantry company.

At the far end of the pond our trail opened into a small clearing. We secured it while helping wet riflemen out of the water. Too small for a Huey, the clearing was just big enough to land a light helicopter. The boss' Korean War-vintage H-13, with room for just him and a pilot, resembled an olive-green gourd with a thick stem attached to the trailing end. My boss alighted. Swapping the commo helmet for my steel pot, I trotted over to meet him, map in hand.

The shooting was soon over. My own company was unscathed. Our job now was to scour the area for the rest of the scattered leg company and get everyone out to the road. It was getting late in the day but we needed less than half an hour to get an accurate head count.

We assigned the leg infantrymen by squad to the corresponding squad tracks of Charlie Company. Our guests were to occupy the squad benches inside the tracks, my men riding on top as usual. The danger of mines was now minimal. We would retrace the same paths our column had already blazed a couple of hours earlier. The two companies, mech and leg, rode together through the north entrance of Lai Khe at nightfall.

The happy ending got me a decoration. I'd cracked into the very temporary ranks of bulletproof combat leaders, a fine laurel for a young captain. A lucky VC/NVA marksman could, of course, revoke this status in the next outing.

Major credit for this "mission accomplished" goes to the man who directed our movements from his flying command post. My boss, Lieutenant Colonel Henry L. Davisson, found the perfect tactic for a seemingly chaotic situation. He simply wrapped the scattered light infantry company in a protective cordon formed by the guns of Charlie Company.

—

* The Third Brigade, First Infantry Division, entered an account of this 4 February action in its General Orders No. 4594 of 19 May 1968. It credited Charlie Company's fires on enemy emplacements for inflicting heavy casualties on an NVA regiment. It also acknowledged casualties in the sister company we extracted.

Chapter 9

The Eyes of Buddha

So adept at stealth were the VC that they often seemed invisible. Yet some innate neural trigger may also alert to impending peril when random sounds, shapes, colors or movements suddenly fuse into a shocking mental mosaic. Some have it, some don't. It's an instinct that keeps soldiers alive.

An operation just west of the Song Dong Nai river and north of the Second Brigade base at Di An included such premonitions of imminent danger. During Tet we moved southeastward into Saigon's northern rice farming suburbs* from Highway 13 after mine-sweeping and clearing some undefended VC brush obstacles on our way through the towns of Lam Son.

Our column of two platoons turned onto a country road that led eastward toward the river. The last hamlet in the settled area was a nondescript string of small thatched-roof hovels built on raised drainage platforms of soil facing the road. So few of the inhabitants were out and about that we assumed they were toiling in the fields or tending their livestock. And, of course, there were no youths of military age.

As our tracks rumbled passed, a slender girl of about twelve years emerged – stark naked – from one of these family houses. Taking no notice of us, she chose to position herself in the morning sunlight near the edge of the dirt platform. Turning her back aloofly, she deliberately squatted to deficate in full view. The mixed expressions on the faces of my soldiers betrayed more shock and embarrassment than wry amusement.

In another war a folk hero had notoriously rendered a similarly symbolic gesture, alone and exposed on the crest of a bald hill in full view of advancing U.S. cavalry. Enraged to be mooned by an insolent savage, the horsemen charged forward – exactly the fatal move he'd intended to provoke. That was Crazy Horse, the gifted aboriginal general whose army of Sioux and Cheyenne warriors later wiped out Custer's 7th Cavalry Regiment on the killing field of Little Big Horn.

Our unabashed pre-adolescent nymphette was no Viet Cong guerilla fighter. But her rude insult left scant doubt for whom she was certainly not rooting in the armed conflict swirling around her home. I had to wonder whether some of her older countrymen would be waiting for us down the road apiece.

A couple of miles further on we entered the area we were ordered to sweep. It was surprising to find a cultured place with stately shade trees, neat bushes and cropped grass but no people. This was a temple sanctuary where birds chirped merrily in serenely picturesque surroundings more like an English garden than the forested war zones we already knew. The gem-like focal point was a small tile-roofed Buddhist shrine made of cut stone.

This peaceful place had a timeless ambience. Even our soldiers respectfully fell silent or spoke in hushed voices. I sent the Second Platoon ahead to scout out what lay beyond a small rise that blocked our view. Dismounting from my track, I inspected the shrine. The gilt and laquered interior was illuminated by burning tapers that charged the air with an aroma like incense.

An old man in ceremonial regalia stood facing me in front of a statue on a raised altar. He had a thin silver beard tapering into a long mandarin goatee. His calm demeanor personified dignity and wisdom. Knowing nothing of Buddhist etiquette, I gave him a slight bow, the palms of my hands pressed together, a gesture he reciprocated. This silent monk spoke no English, making it ridiculous to inquire whether he'd seen any Viet Cong prowling around his quiet precinct. We moved on.

On our left, a hundred yards beyond the shrine, was a spacious Vietnamese cemetery with the typical hollow stone rectangles marking the ancestral graves. For a fleeting instant I glimpsed out of the corner of my eye some vague disturbance on the opposite side of the graveyard where thick hedges began. Whatever it was made no sound and could scarcely be imagined as guerillas in black pajamas. The momentary impression registered more like a undulating cloud of indigo smoke or maybe a flock of dark starlings on the wing, changing shape gracefully against the background of the hedge row.

But I knew in that instant we had company. Immediately I keyed the net to alert both platoon leaders. Seconds later, Two Six radioed back that his men had just made contact on the other side of the small rise that still obscured our view. Heading toward them, my column of tracks went over the rise and down a rugged slope into a vast dry rice paddy where the firefight was in progress.

The Second Platoon's four tracks were clustered out in the rice paddy at the bottom of a heavily wooded hill from which an unseen enemy rained down rifle, automatic and rocket-grenade fire. One of our squads was deployed along the fringe of the steep hillside, the other three already engaged higher up in the woods. The two forces on the covered hillside were so thoroughly entangled in close combat that it was too risky to use our track-mounted heavy machine guns.

To the left of this confused melee was an overgrown ravine that separated the hillside from the high ground at the edge of the cemetery. I sent the First Platoon to work its way on foot into the ravine in order to outflank the enemy. This must have been the ticket because the VC fire soon abated as they retreated to higher ground. The Second Platoon's squads soon emerged from the woods. Wounded men were brought to the tracks in the rice paddy to await dustoff. One of them had his trigger finger shot off at close range.

Two Six described part of the action on the uphill slope. A VC grenade had knocked him flat on his back, semiconscious but still clutching his rifle. An overconfidant enemy soldier, assuming Lt. Stuckey was mortally wounded, reached down to recover the platoon leader's weapon and finish him off with a knife. Some uncanny reflex suddenly made my experienced lieutenant aware of his peril. Still flat on his back he elevated his M-14 with one hand and squeezed off a round into the VC's chest. It was a shot no man could survive for long. I recommended him for a decoration.

His graphic account reminded me of a clash with a rival gang in the ruins of an abandoned bakery back home. What began as a playful teenage duel with hurled chucks of plaster and masonry turned serious when I got in the way of a flying brick. The bleeding head wound taught me a cardinal rule of brick fights: *Ceteris paribus*, fortune favors the gang on the higher ground.

But the First Platoon's sweep of the steep slope quickly disclosed a couple of blood trails leading uphill. The elusive enemy had managed to take his wounded with him. Our men recovered just an abandoned canteen, a backpack, a knife, a couple of ammo web belts and a crude sketch of the area. Brigade intelligence was pleased with the haul. Our body count was more putative.

About a week after this action, Charlie Company was sent again to sweep the same temple complex. It looked different and somehow sad. Still there was the sunny island of bushes, hedge rows and banana palms marking the far horizon of the large dry paddy below the hill. But Rome plows had already been turned loose to level the stately trees that bounded the cemetery on the higher plateau. The ravine had also been torn up but the wooded slope leading down to the rice paddy was almost intact. Too steep for heavy engineer plows.

This time we mostly shunned the little temple and the graveyard, which now seemed naked and defiled without some of their carefully tended plantings. Nothing and no one of interest were found there that day. The timeless little Buddhist shrine had lost its serene charm.

–

*An excellent report of actions before, during and after Tet in the adjacent AO of War Zone D around Saigon is found in *Days of Valor: An Inside Account of the Bloodiest Six Months of the Vietnam War* by Robert L. Tonsetic (Casemate, Philadelphia 2007). It describes intense combat, including urban warfare, involving both mechanized and light infantry units. Also, the book *Sons of Kolchak* by Michael Wikan gives a vivid first-hand account of one straight infantry company's experience in the 25th Infantry Division during the same 1967-1968 period.

Chapter 10

Slaughterhouse in the Sun

A scary Victorian thriller calls for a churchyard and – what else but – "a dark and stormy night". Even Snoopy, the literary pooch in *Peanuts* cartoons, made a playful cliché of that eerie old trope. But if certain tormented souls, cruelly disembodied by foul play, really can't find lasting peace in consecrated ground whatever the weather, there must be legions of them still haunting former battlefields.

Our mounted search for enemy base camps west of Highway 13 took us one day through open woods half a dozen miles north of Lai Khe. Just ahead was a place that was new to us – a couple of treeless acres that glistened brightly under the tropic sun. Closer inspection revealed a level field as silent as a cemetery but far from any human habitation. It was almost completely covered with thousands of bleached white bones.

Most of us knew that our division had spearheaded the huge U.S. deployment to Vietnam in the summer of 1965. A few were also aware that the First Infantry Division fought its first major battle somewhere around here four months later. That showdown on 12 November 1965 went into the annals as the victorious Battle of Bau Bang.

GI stories diverge on what actually happened. But the official name may have been premature because the supposedly chastened insurgents returned to tangle with division again on 20 March 1967 in roughly the same spot. This new action had to be christened the Battle of Bau Bang II. So it gradually dawned on me and my companions that Charlie Company might now be visiting an historic military site.

The bright bones were not yet overgrown. Picked clean, scattered haphazardly and mostly shattered, they would be nearly impossible to reassemble into the skeletons they once were. Some fragments were obviously human, others robust enough to be those of water buffalo or domestic pigs. Badly weathered by long exposure to sun and rain, some of the brittle pieces even showed marks of chewing by wild scavangers.

Together they testified to a sudden, violent death that must have overtaken them just a few years before our visit.

We guessed this to be the result of a savage artillery bombardment, air strikes or both. American units invariably recover the bodies of fallen soldiers, so we took this to be the jumbled remains of Vietnamese livestock and their former owners. Maybe this had been the village of Bau Bang, which survived only on our outdated maps as the nearest place name.

Despite the apparent absence of ghostly intermediaries, this unnatural place imparted a queasy feeling that soon reminded us we had other work to do. We were happy to reenter the fragrant forest of War Zone C. During the series of sweeps in this same operation our mounted procession of armored vehicles ran across another curiousity.

We were following a heading toward what intelligence believed to be an active VC base camp. The lead platoon reported signs of life without specifying what kind. You'll see, said the leader. Glancing to my left through the bushes, I saw a sign facing obliquely toward our passing column, "Stay in Lane" it read in bold, hand-printed, black letters. This was a big, homemade traffic sign on a gray square board held upright by a wooden post about two meters tall, just high enough to fix the gaze of soldiers riding on top of their tracks. The sign was not new.

More misplaced bits of Americana then popped up at intervals of about 50 meters along the line of march, – "No U Turns," ... "Yield Right of Way" ... "Soft Shoulder" ... "No Parking" – as though we somehow had blundered onto old Route 66. I was almost counting on the sixth message to read "Burma-Shave", as it certainly would have on so many U.S. two-lane roads when I was a kid.* But the last sign accurately announced: "Dead End."

No One Home

A lush, dark forest of old growth, the objective of our sweep, now stood in our way. We dismounted the infantry and spread out the tracks in rough formation. A squad soon found a giant tree with a wedge-shaped notch carved into the trunk about knee high. This was pay dirt because the notch, which was just big enough to hold a small candle, had some traces of wax. Two more big trees were found with identical recesses.

The VC were known to do this. A lit candle notched into a tree serves to guide their units returning by night to a camouflaged base camp. The candlelight cannot be detected from the air but is easily spotted by men moving on the ground. So a series of notched trees should form an arc around the camp, telling us how big it might be and betraying a radius pointing toward its center.

Geometry was not much help – too little time and too few candle trees. Our search revealed the camp to be unoccupied. Or maybe the encampment had gone underground in a tunnel network to which we failed to find an entrance. This was a free-fire zone so we reported what we found in case the artillery might like to shell it.

Walking Fish

We took a different route through open woods back to Thunder Road. About half way we came to a huge puddle which probably should not have been there in the dry season. The water was churning with what at first looked like mud skippers. But they must have been lung fish. I told my boss about it. "VC fishpond. Use concussion grenades," he radioed back.

The poor critters were hard to kill. Half a dozen of them started "walking" out of the pond on their stubby fins. The soldiers found this spectacle highly amusing. Somebody said he'd heard that the ungainly fish survive the dry seasons just by burying themselves in the mud, so they must be able to breathe air. The diversion was over when we ran out of walking fish.

Our military reconnaissance played out more like an exotic travelogue. The best part was that we weren't fated this time to take part in the Battle of Bau Bang III. Not a shot was fired nor did any live enemy soldiers pop up in Charlie Company's sights. But I wondered whether a light infantry company would have enjoyed the same luck when poking around that base camp in the forest.

In retrospect, there was nothing very unusual about a fish pond or even the bone yard. But the sequential display of comical traffic signs along our line of march remains a mystery. Monty Python wasn't here. And it's hard to believe that some cosmopolitan Vietnamese once wanted to lure U.S. armor right into their own base camp with a Burma-Shave gimmick. So, it would have to have been the GI whimsy of our own Big Red One brethren on an earlier tour, perhaps in the near aftermath of those battles of Bau Bang. We'll never know.

–

* "Hardly a driver / Is now alive / Who passed / On hills / At 75 / Burma-Shave", read one classic among four decades of those familar roadside commercials that went out of style in 1963.

Chapter 11

Clash of Cultures

Vietnam's hungry cobras like their rats raw but the villagers prefer dogs cooked and served with steamed rice and nuoc mam, a fermented fish sauce for which each family supposedly has a secret recipe. Raiding a base camp, we once captured a VC canteen full of this smelly, dark brown brew. It was delicious.

Nevertheless, roast rack of Rover remained too exotic for GI tastes. We watched with curiosity one day as a frail old man, club in hand concealed behind his back, offered a morcel of chicken foot to a stray yellow mongrel. One swift thump on the noggin was all it took before he grabbed up the limp hind legs and carried the incautious mutt off to his nearby house for supper.

This was the village of Phuoc Cuong astride Highway 13, halfway between Lai Khe and Saigon. Children frolicking in the road slowed our armored column and a couple vendors seized the chance to make a sale. One offered a new looking AK-47 for four of our tempermental M-16s, a bargain price in my opinion. Another had a bundle of long baguettes. The one I purchased wasn't as appetizing as it looked. Too much gritty sand had gotten in the dough and the taste was way too bland to pass for metropolitan French.

A little farther on a white chauffeured Mercedes cabriolet, convertible top down, containing an middle-aged European in a tan safari outfit and white straw hat, passed us on its way north to Lai Khe. The distinguished gent waved. It was Peter Scholl-Latour, the veteran German-French war correspondent and globe-trotting author of *Death in the Rice Paddy* and *Eyewitness: Vietnam*.

A search & destroy mission just to the East of this place included an awkward intercultural exchange between the former French colonial subjects and their latest Western liberators. We headed up a dirt road past a wide farm plot. A burst of small arms fire came out of a rubber plantation just ahead as the lead APC ran over a landmine. The track's crew was furious. A squad rushed the rubber in futile pursuit of the fleeing insurgents.

The angry squad leader spotted a suspect in a conical hat still obliviously puttering in his field fifty yards away. The skinny old farmer was frog-marched onto the road at gunpoint. The squad returning from the rows of rubber trees had found telltale sandal marks and footprints of the guerrillas who had been been setting up the roadblock.

When I got there, my guys were trying Dick Tracy-style to determine whether the diminutive horticulturalist's bare feet fit those enemy prints next to the disabled track. The terrified farmer obviously hadn't a clue what the irate Americans wanted from him. He must have surmised from the shouting and pointing that they expected him to dance about.

Somewhere I'd seen this slapstick routine before. Bingo, it was a western film's bar-room scene in which some drunken cowboys entertained themselves by shooting their revolver bullets at the boots of California, Hopalong Cassidy's bewhiskered sidekick. The harmless old mountain man had committed the gaffe of ordering a sarsparilla in their saloon, prompting the hooligans to make him pay for that sissified blunder by doing some Bojangles jumps and leaps.

Like Hoppy, I intervened. It was enough to point out diplomatically that the barefoot Vietnamese looked too frail even to pick up a mine or dig a hole for it. Track fixed, we spared that old gray head and marched on to win some more minds and hearts.

Ambush

Charlie Company returned to Lai Khe for a stand-down in mid-February. That made us part of the force defending the big base that was being sporadically shelled. The job included assigning armored infantry escorts for various tasks required by the brigade and the division. There were enough daily missions that elements of our unit sometimes needed to be parcelled out piecemeal.

The strength of a security force depended upon the probable threat. I underestimated the level of enemy activity just south of Lai Khe, since there was an ARVN garrison only about three miles down the road at Ben

Cat. So it was on 18 February when the division engineers had to run a column of M-88 tank retrievers and heavy equipment down Highway 13 to Di An, a brigade base just north of Saigon.

A couple of Charlie Company's mounted squads from the Second Platoon, the paramedic track, our two attached M-48A1 tanks from the 4/64 Armor and some military police vehicles were detailled to ride shotgun. The engineers' M-88s, large boxy track-recovery vehicles, were also well armed with heavy M-2 guns.

Somewhere south of Ben Cat the column encountered a roadblock, a fairly common nuisance on this stretch of Highway 13 during Tet. We would normally remove the obstacles and our soldiers would sweep the road around them for mines. Nothing lost but time. But this engineer column soon came under fire from the East side of the road. There were casualties.

The .50 caliber gunner on the medic track was among them. This soldier from Tennessee had taken a bullet through his helmet that spun around and exited again, leaving a nasty path of scalp lacerations, recalled Sp5 James Perlmutter, the senior medic who was sitting an arm's length away in the track commander's position. Also among the casualties he attended was a warrant officer and the rest of an injured crew inside a targeted M-88. A dustoff helicopter evacuated the wounded but the ambush was far from over.

The division had to reinforce with part of its attached First Squadron, Fourth Armored Calvary Regiment. Air Force jets swooped in, dropping napalm canisters on the enemy force. The action lasted the rest of the day. The beleaguered engineer column with its ad hoc security never made it to Di An; it returned to Lai Khe. Charlie Company's senior medic, who eventually retired as a colonel of the Medical Corps, was awarded a Silver Star for his cool performance under fire. The citation said 84 enemy soldiers were killed in that battle.

This farming area north of Saigon remained a hot spot during Tet. Alpha Company, our 2/2 sister unit, exchanged fire with some VC hidden in a five-acre patch of woods in the middle of a vast rice paddy at the start of the rainy monsoon. Charlie Company was making its own sweep not far from the southern side of that woods, and Daring Six hoped to trap the VC with a pincer movement – Alpha blocking the North side, Charlie advancing from the South.

I went into the woods with one platoon. We found a well camouflaged watch tower, a bit of equipment and various signs of occupation. But there was no further shooting and no more VC to be seen. They must have decided to wait us out underground. This place was so thickly jungled that we could have whiled away many happy hours just looking for the tunnel entrance.

That news couldn't have pleased Daring Six, who was circling like a mad hornet in his little command chopper, looking for something else to sting. He who-must-be-obeyed broke squelsh; my RTO handed me the set, the angry growling being for me: "Charlie Six, Daring Six. Your One-Six element has got a track stuck out in the middle of the rice paddy and IT'S SINKING OUT OF SIGHT! Get over there right now and recover that track.

Disengaging from thorn bushes, I hastened to my APC to find the offending First Platoon. The next message from the boss beat me to it: "I want that platoon leader relieved on the spot." The relatively new platoon leader assured me on the company net that there was no crisis. Sure enough, the wet track was still in the mud when I got there. But the lieutenant and his men somehow managed to get it out under its own steam. We then had a chat face to face.

Every combat leader affects a masque of command. That of Daring Six, who had been brigade boxing champion in his cadet days, was a convincing mix of tough and gruff. I was always more scared to cross him than I ever was of the VC and NVA. But my boss actually had a heart of gold. His top priority was the welfare of his men. His concern for his young officers was genuine. Seeing no gain from firing my otherwise promising platoon leader, I bet on Daring Six forgetting the sinking-track episode. Which he did.

Pompous princeling

Sometime during Tet we returned to Thunder IV. A field-force general dropped in for a meeting with the light infantry battalion CO there and dispatched his new aide to inspect our perimeter. This captain in fancy tailored fatigues and shined boots collared me with vital instructions from on high. He wanted a written report on improving our defenses and a scenario on how we'd deal with a hypothetical attack by a large force – as though that possibility had never occurred to us. For example, supposed it came from there, he said, pointing vaguely toward the woodline to the West.

Fine, I replied, that's just where the assault actually came from when we beat off a reinforced NVA battalion here last December. The defenses you see in front of you worked as planned. My company built them. But I did learn to insist that every soldier must sleep under mortar-proof overhead cover, as you can now see. I omitted mention of the only hitch in our defense – remote radio meddling from the rear, which cost us a patrol. The officious new staff officer had never even heard of that action anyway. He and his general soon flew off to pester the next Thunder base. No hypothetical reports ever got written.

Shortly thereafter we were told to go fortify a virgin base location before nightfall after breaking down good old Thunder IV, which was getting a bit squalid. It took hours to empty and retrieve the sandbags, roll up the concertina wire and stow the stuff on the tracks. The M-113s and M48A1 tanks backed out of their trenches, revealing packs of rats that had been living in and around the puddles and refuse in the dug-in vehicle fighting positions. Our local cobras must have been on strike.

Big, healthy, well fed and multi-colored, the rats were temporarily disoriented by the glare of sunlight when departing armored vehicles deprived them of their subterranean comfort zone. They offered good target practice with a .45. We shot a few rodents. This being the bitter end of Thunder IV, the poor critters reminded me of a more deserving target – a thoughtless rat with a radio.

–

Chapter 12

Trouble Shooting

The deadliest threat to the young men in our fire base wasn't always incoming bullets, rockets or mortar rounds from an enemy lurking outside. A shadow of doom could also invade our camp, arriving by helicopter, if the morning mail pouch contained a devastating Dear John letter from home.

Late one afternoon in Thunder IV there was a muffled explosion. A thin whisp of gray smoke betrayed the source – one entrenched sleeping position protected partly by a covering of sandbags. In it lay the horribly mangled body of a young, black soldier, his chest and hands now looking more like a dark mass of bloody hamburger meat.

We also found the perfumed letter over which he'd been brooding for hours before extracting the pin from a hand grenade he had deliberately held over his broken heart. His closest comrade knew about the letter. But he couldn't anticipate how this untimely blow to a private dream of future bliss would rob his buddy of the will to live.

Why didn't the man confide his profound disappointment? The army trains leaders to pay heed to all sorts of problems that may affect a unit's morale. Maybe this was the rare personal tragedy beyond any realistic command intervention.

A newly assigned squad leader once came to me with a more familiar dilemma: Sir, I'm detailled to lead tonight's ambush patrol. I can't do it. I'm afraid, he said. Tall, fair, athletically built, he had been a collegiate football hero before he was caught in the draft. Now he was a junior NCO who looked every inch the model soldier.

Everyone's afraid, I told him, rolling out the standard command pep talk: That's normal. The trick is to tackle inner fears rationally. You've got the training to overcome them. Just focus your mind on those men in the patrol who are depending upon your leadership.

But that's exactly the problem, he explained. My fear is so overpowering that it makes it impossible for me to move. I know myself. I'd just freeze up from terror out there. I wouldn't be able to take action and my patrol could be lost. I can't do it.

He was intelligent, well spoken and convincing. I also believed he was sincere. And that made it my problem. I'm no mark. But this man just wasn't cut out to function as an infantry squad leader. I had the first sergeant get him reassigned the next day. The man thanked me.

Without consistent leadership an army filled with conscripts takes pot luck. Our division had a staffing advantage, I heard, because some of its own were now running the Pentagon's personnel desk. Our young soldiers really were a cut above the ones I'd previously dealt with in the European command where the best men were being drawn down for Vietnam.

There were rare exceptions. One was a handsome red-haired rascal who was temporarily parked with us pending court-martial for desertion, among other felonies. During a raid on an enemy base camp I observed that he was no coward. I was also surprised to learn that he could read the Vietnamese notes found there, having enjoyed his AWOL stint among the natives, girls especially. Language talent was useful to us and brigade intelligence. Too bad he wasn't around when we captured other VC documents, along with a batch of letters penned by a GI defector. But, of course, those letters were already in English.

Not long afterward, the first sergeant handed me a fresh charge sheet against the soldier, this time for homosexual rape. The pathetic sodomy victim was an undersized conscript who was the mental and physical inferior of this slick predator, who probably would have mounted a female water buffalo if it struck his fancy. We turned him over to the military police. He would probably be just as much a danger to fellow inmates at Fort Leavenworth military prison as he would be on any city street. Under other circumstances, his street-smart intellect and manipulative grasp of human nature might have been the right amoral ingredients for a high-flying career in politics.

Around Christmas time in an NDP east of Lam Son my troops were busy cleaning their weapons. A shot was heard, followed by a painful howl. A young private had managed to shoot off a toe with his M-16. He asked to see me a few days after his return from medical treatment in Lai Khe. He told me his two problems and asked whether I might help him. I heard him out, since he was a good troop, according to his squad and platoon leaders, and he had never been in any trouble.

Firstly, he feared receiving an Article 15, non-judicial punishment, for ignoring the Army's iron-clad safety rules on weapon handling. The accident was hard to explain to himself, he said, because he thought he had conscientiously followed the well-rehearsed procedure. Yet, he had to agree with me that an M-16, clean or dirty, can scarcely fire a bullet if the chamber has first been cleared as required.

Secondly, he was hoping to make a career in the army and feared that disciplinary action might spike his scheduled promotion to private first class. Naturally, he'd been looking forward to the pay boost. I told him my options were limited but that I was not unsympathetic and would get back to him after a chat with the first sergeant. I believe a mutually satisfactory compromise was found.

We lost two experienced mortar gunners, one at Lorraine II during Shenandoah II in October and the other about three months later in one of the Thunder NDPs. Both men were hurt in the heat of contact fire missions while feeding projectiles into their tubes as quickly as possible. Each man lost most of a thumb and his first two or three fingers. The digits were sheared off by the fins of a new round being dropped into the tube just as another one came blasting out of it. The incidents were nearly identical. Can these be called accidents?

Gunners train to pump out rounds as quickly as they can during enemy contact missions. The manual contains no cautionary language against "too fast." The rhythmic motion and rote pattern of feeding the tubes should ensure the appropriate time lag. The previous projectile should have cleared the tube, unless the bags of propellent charge between its fins were defective.

The division had acknowledged such an issue in October when a mortar's short round struck our listening post. We had apparently received outdated ammunition that had become wet in storage at some point. It seems likely that this was the cause, namely the propellent charge fizzed off more slowly than it was designed to do. Whatever the case, I'm convinced our two maimed gunners were faithfully following the officially prescribed loading procedure.

The constant interaction of fallible men with explosive ordnance makes accidents inevitable. Everyone in our mech battalion knew the cautionary mid-1967 tale of the munition-laden track that blew up when a soldier jumped down from the cargo hatch, triggering an armed claymore mine someone had already prepared and laid out on the track floor. A claymore blasting cap also went off inside one of our vehicles one evening but we managed to escape those fatal consequences.

A new platoon leader was assigned to Charlie Company toward the end of my tour on line. He was a hard charger who waded into his job with obvious enthusiasm. One day his platoon drew a mission just south of Lai Khe near Ben Cat and the Iron Triangle, notorious for VC underground networks. A tunnel entrance was discovered and the men tried their luck playing tunnel rats.

When it came time to leave, the tunnel was rigged for demolition with C4 explosive charges. They could be set off with lengths of cord, giving the men time to take cover before the blast. The fuse was lit. The men waited. Nothing happened. Overcome by impatience, the platoon leader went to see what was wrong. The overdue explosion greeted him at the tunnel entrance.

I missed that operation but was briefed on the outcome. The impetuous lieutenant was showered by pieces of tunnel and suffered a broken arm, accidental injuries that weren't life threatening. An account tinged with *Schadenfreude* circulated in the ranks that he might face an Article 15 for damaging government property, namely himself.*

We also respected civilian property. Looting was taboo. During a smoke break after searching a hamlet in Lam Son I spotted a soldier sitting on a beautifully carved, red lacquered cermonial stool. I could have locked his heels while reciting the dire disciplinary consequences he faced.

Instead, I admired his trophy, noting that U.S. Customs would demand to see his purchase receipt to calculate the import tariff if he tried to ship such a bulky item home through the mails. I also pointed out that the VC we were were trying to flush from the hamlet would gain one more recruiting argument if the locals complained that their village had been plundered by U.S. troops. He and I agreed that he would now put the stool back exactly where he "found" it, since our column wouldn't move one inch until that happened.

—

* Our platoon leader shared the same name as a contemporary who later retired with three stars.

Chapter 13

An Uncertain Trumpet

"Don't knock the war, sir. It's the only one we've got", my first sergeant remarked, feigning seriousness. The soldiers out of earshot of my casual conversation with Top might have wondered what he and the Old Man were laughing about. Pretty soon the whole world knew.

It was the end of March 1968. Charlie Company, awaiting its next combat mission, was busy cleaning and maintaining equipment in Thunder II, a spiffy War Zone C base we had recently built all for ourselves. A resupply helicopter had dropped off its cargo, including current and back issues of *Stars & Stripes*.

There we read of rising antiwar sentiment at home. Yes, and it looked like domestic fallout from the Tet offensive was also causing President Johnson to think twice about seeking a new term in the White House.

We knew that a distraught Robert McNamara had deserted his Pentagon post as the civilian architect of the war effort. Now the paper said LBJ had replaced him with an elite, formerly hawkish Washington lawyer named Clark Clifford. An astute political columnist profiled the man as a Democrat insider who'd gone dovish and might favor a face-saving U.S. disengagement.

I harbored no illusion about how such an abrupt policy reversal might affect our own mission in Vietnam. Even though the Tet offensive was being crushed, between these printed lines it read like the brave hearts and minds on the Potomac were openly beating retreat or toppling like dominoes. Could it be that the government that put us here was now contemplating a plan to abandon its own army in the field?

This was the topic of my conversation with First Sergeant Elam, an intelligent Texan who had seen a lot of strange things in almost two decades in the U.S. Army. Troops always grouse, but as he and other senior NCOs so often quip: A grousing troop is a happy troop. The Old Man, his junior by at least ten years, was still happy, just a tad concerned at the breaking news.

We both knew what made young soldiers tick. It occurred to us that from this moment onward teenaged conscripts plucked off the farms and streets of America might have some misgivings about the risks they could face in a distant conflict that was now being repudiated by their families, friends, neighbors and the country's exalted figures of authority.

Top and I killed some time by pencilling on the back of a C-rations carton roughly what we knew of our order of battle in Vietnam. With victory always lurking just around the corner, Gen. Westmoreland, our supreme commander, had asked for another 200,000 troops. And the news reports spoke of some 550,000 troops already under his command now – the peak of the troop buildup.

We figured roundly that at any given time there could not have been more than 55,000 of us in the infantry and armored cavalry maneuver elements in direct contact with the foe on the ground in Vietnam (not counting maybe another 30,000 in supporting artillery, engineer and signal units). Those 55,000 were the vital organs of twelve divisions.

This sounds impressive since a standard U.S. division boasts around 16,000 men. And such a division fields ten maneuver battalions, each with some 600 or more men, at least on paper, although some of those men aren't included in actual combat formations.

Together, all these maneuver battalions – armored infantry, armored cavalry, light infantry – can be considered the teeth of Westy's fighting pit bull. Now compare that snarling jaw of roughly 55,000 marching GIs with the peak theater strength of more than half a million men under arms. Actually, chances of any Vietnam-bound soldier drawing a line infantry job were known to be about one in eight. What were the other seven doing? Our simple arithmetic revealed that – presto! – our huge logistical tail was ten times as robust as the combat jaws of our aenemic pit bull.

We had also heard that the enemy cleverly inverted the shape of our Potemkin colossus. Our bloated 9:1 support vs. combat ratio was exactly the reverse, namely 1:9 for the scrappy natives out there in the woods taking potshots at us. As Dwight Eisenhower once said, "It's not the size of the dog in the fight, but the size of the fight in the dog." Of course, Ike was right. He knew about "mass" as a principle of war. But maybe he was thinking of a different army.

Any young man unlucky enough to be drafted after Tet should have grasped that his government had basically deserted the urgent geopolitical cause it had trumpeted when sending its army into Vietnam. That awareness would soon have severe repercussions for morale. Within less than a year, new phenomena like fragging, desertion, even troop mutinies, began to generate ugly new headlines back home. Apparently, some of our countrymen just hadn't grasped that the U.S. Army did not send itself off to Indochina.

Washington's political loss of nerve eroded esteem for the armed forces. But the next couple of decades without serious wars permitted government and the Pentagon gradually to spruce up the public image of the military. The draft ended. Media blossomed out with inspiring support-the-troops coverage. Patriotism came back in vogue. Pretty soon most Americans were eager to thank just about anyone in uniform for his or her service – a stellar PR achievement, despite the disappearance of the country's only credible foreign adversary, the Soviet Union. Orchestrated cheerleading for the armed services probably peaked toward the end of the 20th Century as a series of easier wars were quietly taking shape on the planning board.

Aging Vietnam veterans were especially surprised to be received into the pantheon of national role models, sometimes even celebrated as heroes. The Pentagon had noted long ago that only about three million men, some who went back for a second or even third Vietnam tour, had been dispatched to Indochina during the years of heaviest U.S. involvement, 1965-1972. A nationwide survey by a polling organization compared that old number with something entirely new. It found that 13 million American men were now claiming to be proud Vietnam War veterans.

Had the Pentagon somehow lost track of about 800 U.S. divisions? Or were 10 million vicarious warriors just taking a cue from their leaders and media? Perhaps the ranks of this ghost legion – like their last four presidents at this present moment – had better things to do in their youth.

Six months before Top and I casually tallied up our convoluted economy of force, the Big Red One urgently circulated an affidavit to all its officers.

This was the division's response to a damaging *New York Times* report describing the photographed mutilation of the body of a slain Viet Cong guerrilla. The commanding general had been called on the carpet, his division's reputation sullied by an eyewitness account that then rippled sensationally across all domestic media coverage.

The scandal fizzled when it was turned out that the reporter and photographer on the scene had innocently asked to see how we cut off a VC's ears and even supplied a naive soldier with the knife. The September 1967 division affidavit made clear it was never the division's policy to mutiliate any corpses under any circumstances.

Without the slightest whiff of command influence, this was unanimously endorsed by all serving officers. I was proud to sign. But the self-styled newspaper of record had cleverly positioned itself in the media vanguard of the nascent war protests. Mission accomplished.

There were plenty of U.S. war correspondents with the Big Red One in 1965 and 1966 but hardly any after this flap. We saw none of them in the next seven months, although a reporter for a Korean news agency came along on one of our sweeps. An officer with another division gained a similar impression of media reporting from Vietnam: "In early '66 in the 1st Cav we had all kinds of American, British, etc. following us around the highlands. Six months later all you saw in the field were Korean and Filippino camera crews. The American reporters were doing voice-overs from the restaurant on top of the Caravelle Hotel where they were headquartered."

Naturally, such rare excursions into the realm of strategy and policy were way above our working infantry pay grade. Charlie Company at the end of March found itself attached to our regimental sister battalion, the First Battalion, Second Infantry. It's commander, LTC Mortimer O'Connor had notched accolades as "the hero of Bu Dop" for winning a big fight next to the Cambodian border to our northeast. From school days, I knew him as my "plebe pop", which is what we called West Point faculty officers assigned as informal sponsors of a group of young cadets.

This time his light infantry battalion – call sign: Dracula – was suddenly sent off on a new mission. His soldiers wore black neckerchiefs as their mark of esprit. We then heard that Dracula Six had been shot through the heart on 1 April in an ambush after his battalion was helicoptered into a contested landing zone. He left a wife and seven children.

I spent a week in Hong Kong in early April when my turn for R&R finally came up. My own battalion commander dropped by my NDP with some devastating news when I returned. While I was gone, my friend and classmate, Capt. Robert Serio, had been killed instantly in a fight on 17 April while leading his armored unit of the First Squadron, Fourth Armored Cavalry, assigned to the First Infantry Division.

Serio and I grew up in the northeast Bronx, attended rival Catholic high schools and were both appointed to the academy by the same local congressman in 1960. He was a born leader, excelling in athletics and academics. His talent was so obvious that many of us assumed he would be among the first to prove the "stars in store" motto Gen. Westmoreland had coined for our class of 1964.

We had chatted and quaffed beer a couple of evenings in mid-March at Lai Khe when my company was working for the 1/4 Cav as division reserve. He was then assistant operations officer of the "Quarter Cav", the man who passed me my order for the next day. Bob was bored with his staff job, saying how desperately he wanted to take command of a cavalry troop and that he envied me for having my own company. On 17 April, about two weeks after he got his wish, his luck ran out.

—

Chapter 14

Homecoming

Not even Hänsel and Gretel could have gone lost in our wooded, mostly flat region of Vietnam, even though there were very few conspicuous terrain features for visual orientation. Land navigation to a military objective usually meant following a compass heading blindly for as long as it took to get there. On rare occasions, though, trouble arose because our designated objective was somehow bewitched.

The danger of a human error in fixing a location can be open-ended. We could, for example, inadvertently tangle with a friendly unit in the woods or stray into an area being targeted by our own artillery or bombers. Our intramural gunplay near the Song Dong Nai showed how faulty timing can also ruin a decent plan. Two more outings described below were apparently jinxed by misinformation.

The objective of a sweep or a search-&-destroy mission typically reached us by radio in the form of coded map coordinates. We used old French survey maps with a metric grid overprinted with more recent mosaics of CIA aerial photography. Thanks to different methods of projection, the two images sometimes failed to line up. Occasionally this would reveal, for example, a misplaced intermittent stream somehow flowing uphill or a road that wasn't quite where it should have been. But these were minor glitches for which we could easily adjust.

Apart from de rigueur radio encryption codes and a field notebook, a company commander never moved without a trusty lensatic compass, a waterproof watch and his map in a clear, plastic, waterproof case on which he would mark the assigned coordinates and route with a grease pencil. For a complex operation he might also receive an overlay sketch that could be inserted into the map case precisely over the correct part of the map and then removed after he traced its details onto the outside of the case with the grease pencil.

One time in April encoded coordinates arrived by radio. They marked a search objective almost due west of our NDP on Thunder Road halfway between Lai Khe and Loc Ninh. We started early because the destination was several miles through the woods. A civilian flatbed truck with a crew of loggers soon crossed our column's path on an unmarked trail. This was a bit unusual because one of the crewmen was obviously not Vietnamese. I assumed the fair, blue-eyed Occidental who greeted me with a nod must be a Frenchman working for some local rubber plantation.

We were mostly able to plow through the open woods and brush without dismounting. The exception was the occasional encounter with Indochina's red ants. These vicious insects make nests in the trees by somehow gluing a couple of adjacent leaves together in a pod. A shower of angry ants rains down when a track antenna disturbs an overhead nest. Each ant instinctively aims to anchor its pincers in GI skin. These bites are painful, so everyone on the track jumps up, shucks clothing and begins smacking ants. Such single combat has even been known to interrupt fire fights. And the head of a dismembered ant never relaxes its pincer lock until it is physically extracted from the skin.

Apart from the C-rations lunch break, another thing that can stop a column is the predictable effect of the malaria pills, namely diarrhea. Every soldier carries a packet or two of GI toilet paper in case he has to dart into the bushes. But leaves will do in a pinch, there being no poison ivy in Vietnam. Come my turn, ample security was posted. Even the vigilant coterie of mandarins attending the last boy emperor of China never rendered such protection as the guns of Charlie Company.

We were making good time but still had a couple of miles to go by mid-afternoon. Even if we didn't find an enemy force at our objective, I thought we still might have to overnight in the forest. At that point came an angry radio call from Daring Six. Charlie Six, where the hell are you? I gave him our location in shackle code, which substitutes letters for numbers. Christ on a crutch, he erupted, that's nowhere near where you were supposed to go. What the hell are you doing there? You're lost.

We're following the most direct heading to our objective, said I. Rubbish! said the boss. He demanded to know what objective I was talking about. I shackled the coordinates battalion had radioed to me the previous evening. Wait, he said. There was a long pause. Daring Six came up again, this time with a more composed, You're right. I couldn't resist a smug I-told-you-so zinger. No reply. But he ordered me to turn the company around and get back to the NDP ASAP.

That suited me fine. I reckoned us to be within five miles of the Cambodian border salient and we'd now be unlikely to reach our NDP before nightfall. I never did learn what went wrong with the radioed coordinates. But I was glad to be far from the boss' command post staff when he tracked down the source of the snafu. Except for our droning engines, the forest of War Zone C was pleasantly quiet on the way back.

We kept the battalion posted on our progress, the last couple of miles running slowly in the dark. The lights suddenly came on again. They were dozens of parachute flares fired continually by an artillery battery at the boss' request. Was this a neat way to say: Welcome Home? Touching, almost. I recalled how my mother left the back porch light burning at our hillside summer cabin so I could pick my way back through the woods after night angling for small-mouth bass on the lake in the valley.

The Quiet Village

A subsequent mission in April featured a more mysterious glitch. This time Charlie Company was scrambled to recapture a village we were told had been taken over by a large force of VC and NVA. That task was passed down to our battalion from the brigade or division. We were the closest available unit. So, I issued a warning order to the leaders and went off to attempt a visual reconnaissance from a distance.

This village was only a mile or two east of Highway 13. I'd never seen it before, so let's call it Village X. We were supposed to approach from the south by moving through a wide-open rice paddy that was at least three miles long south to north. The South side of the village was protected by a long earthen berm. Habitations were barely visible above the berm, suggesting that the settlement sloped downward north of that point. I envisaged rows of thatched hooches stretching along dirt streets, a tough nut to crack if a stubborn enemy was ensconced in the buildings as we had to assume. But at least there was plenty of daylight left.

Before EDT departure I had time to issue the standard five-paragraph field order to the platoon leaders. This operation promised to be a doozy and we wanted everyone pumped up for it. Excitement filled the air. The platoon leaders rushed off to brief their infantry squads, which would be the first to go over the berm when the assault began. House-to-house combat was on the cards.

The first couple of miles we rode in column, fourteen APCs and two M48A1 tanks raising a long cloud of pale yellow dust. In the last 500 yards, Charlie Company took up its planned attack formation. Hoping for surprise, my plan was to hold our fire until we drew fire from the village. The First and Second Platoons swung on line left and right along the length of the berm, the Third Platoon behind them in a staggered column, ready to punch through the middle as the assault developed. This final mounted battle formation resembled a giant T. From the air it must have made a glorious sight.

Counting on the 90-mm tank guns with high-explosive ordnance to blast holes in the berm, I deployed my tanks closest to the central point between the two platoons on line. My command track and the medic track advanced just to the left of center. Since the berm was about five feet high and 300 yards long, the tracks of our mech assault line covered most of it. Adrenaline was surging. Obviously the advantage of surprise was ours.

At the 200-yard mark, the battalion net suddenly crackled to life with the urgent voice of Daring Six: BREAKER, Breaker! Check fire, Halt the attack now, I say again, Halt the attack. I echoed the command on my net. We collectively crumbled pathetically like a jumbo jet somehow blowing all its tires on the last stage of a transatlantic takeoff. The free-fall crash from do-or-die elan to wheel-spinning confusion was deflating for all of us.

That was my last outing with all of Charlie Company together. I never did learn what went awry, The way my taciturn battalion commander packaged it, intelligence must have gotten the status of the village wrong. Were we just tilting at phantoms? Maybe, but the absolute last-minute correction leaves room for more questions.

Did Village X really contain innocent farmers who had been infiltrated by armed insurgents? If so, even an accidental salvo of gunfire from behind the berm could have triggered a huge bloodbath. That occurred to me later when reading reports of what happened to a village called My Lai.

Were there really any Vietnamese civilians behind that berm? I still wonder. Is it possible that someone circling in a chopper wanted to witness or maybe film a classical armored infantry charge reminiscent of Europe during World War II? Can't rule it out in retrospect. But the maneuvering combat formation Charlie Company put on display in this dry rice paddy had to be an absolute rarity for Vietnam. Almost like film taken from an old war documentary, it was truly a sight to behold.

There was a deadly postscript late in my last month in command. I had sent one platoon northward from Lai Khe to guard a nearby section of Highway 13. A new lieutenant from Arkansas was in charge. He had spread out his tracks along the road's shoulder near the dense woods. One squad was surprised by a burst of small arms fire and a blast that hit their track. It must have been an RPG 7, which can penetrate the aluminum armor with a shape charge, causing deadly interior spalling. Only the driver was still inside.

Lt. McCarty alerted me while rushing to the stricken APC. He was the first to crawl inside it just as l got there. His face was pale and he was visible sickened when he emerged. Nothing could be done for the mangled track driver. The stealthy VC armor-killing team had escaped unseen. This was a new officer's initiation to mech infantry in Vietnam.

—

Chapter 15

Happy Camping

About thirty years ago I was visiting my brother on Hawaii and he introduced a friend who was a Vietnam veteran. The friend was familiar with Big Red One territory because his support command ran convoys along Highway 13. He even recalled having to bivouac with his crew temporarily in the closest Thunder base when an accident disabled an overloaded truck.

He went on to describe that NDP as the most hospitable lodging he'd experienced on his entire 1968-1969 tour. Apart from the stout defenses, he was especially impressed with the impregnable command bunker, roofed with mortar-proof layers of sandbags and shored up with sturdy timbers. The place was even big enough for a poker table, making him regret having to depart so soon.

Voila! That sounded just like Thunder II — a name he easily recalled when I guessed it. You know who built it? I asked, pointing to myself. I'm glad you liked our accommodations. Good taste. And you know what? Our deputy division commander for operations once confided that Thunder II was the real pearl in the division's long string of Thunder bases along Highway 13.

The posh command bunker we owed to a different convoy mishap that occurred practically right in front of Thunder II in early April 1968, shortly after Charlie Company, 2/2, built the place. Some telephone poles spilled unnoticed off a flatbed trailer and my first sergeant sent our men out to scavange them after the convoy passed. That's where all the sturdy carpentry came from.

A few days after that lumber bonanza, I was surprised to get a radio call from Danger 79. He said he had just flown over our base and wanted to take a closer look, if we would kindly secure a landing place for his C&C helicopter. Why not? We were standing tall. He'd obviously spotted our chopper landing pad protected by its own wall of concertina wire just outside the base's northern perimeter. I went out with a squad to escort our VIP visitor into the inner sanctum.

After admiring our spacious command bunker, the general marveled that Thunder II was laid out in perfect symmetry when viewed from above. He wanted to know how we did that. I proudly explained the geometry:

The company posted security after choosing a virgin level site that could be easily defended. I stood at the center with a mortar aiming circle on a tripod, measuring off sequentially three arcs of 120 degrees as the line platoon sectors. Platoon sergeants and soldiers with engineer stakes then marked my assigned boundaries on the perimeter. Within the sectors we also staked out positions for each squad's machine gunner and for the rifleman. Then the men began digging their Hays holes, filling sandbags and clearing fields of fire. Even the outer barbed wire was partly up before nightfall.

My VIP guest was obviously appreciating my guided tour of Charlie Company's gorgeously geometric perimeter defenses. But then somehow – I wonder whether its an innate instinct possessed only by flag officers – his gaze was magnetically attracted to something ... irregular. Oh my God, I thought; this can't be happening now!

Sanitation had very recently become a priority with the division and maybe the whole field-force command. All field bases were now supposed to have proper toilets, namely old 55-gallon drums, sawed in half and partly filled with diesel fuel that could be burned off hygienically every few days, a new directive said. A cargo helicopter had even dropped off a wooden outhouse structure to place over our fecal collection tubs. No more unsightly slit-trenches were allowed in the bases, by order of the division commander.

"What is that installation?" asked the general as he approached for closer inspection. "It .. err .. Sir, it looks like .. err .. it might be a ... ," I croaked with dismay. And sure enough, lying resplendently there at the bottom of the unauthorized two-foot-deep retangular excavation we were now peering into was – what else but – a fresh turd.

Danger Seven Niner did not comment. But he seemed to loose interest in the striking martial beauty of Thunder II. I saluted and he flew off to continue his inspection of lesser Thunder encampments.

Life in the field bases could become fairly civilized. To shave in the morning, men would fill their steel helmets with water. At Thunder IV, there had been a stream from which water for cooking or washing could be pumped into a tank and sterilized. Elsewhere, water tanks could be trucked or flown in. Tablets to disinfect water were part of a soldier's kit, as were salt tablets, essential for dismounted operations in the blazing tropic heat.

The shower was simplicity itself. Place a platform of duck board on the ground beside an APC and an inverted five-gallon can of water head-high above it on a horizontal board with its other end counter-balanced atop the vehicle by some sand bags. Stand on the duck board under the can and open the water cap a bit. Uncle Sam's soap was free.

Laundry was done at Lai Khe. There wasn't too much to launder since no one wore underwear. The basic uniform was light, baggy, jungle-fatigue trousers and matching blouse with the sleeves rolled up. The olive-green jungle boots of canvass mesh and leather had little eyelet ports just above the soles so that water drained out during the wet season. Embedded in the thick rubber soles was a plate of flat metal to protect against punji stakes.

Huge black rubber bladders of APC diesel fuel were flown in. Sometimes we stored the empties for pickup outside the wire. One of those at Thunder IV was vandalized overnight. A clever Vietnamese with a sharp knife had carved out of it a spiffy new pair of rubber flip-flops.

Each Thunder also had a garbage pit outside the wire. Civilians of all ages would travel up the road to scavange the GI trash in the daylight hours. One man's trash, another man's treasure.

Mech infantry spent so much time in the field bases that money was superfluous. My basic monthly expense was a couple of *dong* banknotes for the elderly Vietnamese barber who made the round of bases. But during convoy security duty some of the men contracted business and more with the Lambretta girls working the road. About once a month, a medical team would come to the NDP with penicillin shots against venereal diseases. Then there would be a lineup of soldiers dropping their trousers in turn and bending over.

Marijuana was also on sale on the road. Whenever that became a problem, the first sergeant would organize a shakedown of the troops for contraband. Alcoholic drinks and radios were not permitted in the bases. But C-ration cartons usually contained cigars or cigarettes.

We've all heard the famous aphorism about an army travelling on its stomach. Decent food is an obvious morale factor and the U.S. Army spared no expense to provide it. Bravo Six and I compared notes on that score since both of us placed heavy emphasis on the quality of the company mess in the field. Charlie Company went through three mess teams during my tenure, one very talented crew bloodied in December's night attack, the next sent packing by my first sergeant for substandard chow. We eventually got the quality line soldiers deserved. Compared with the dismal fare served at the brigade staff officers mess in Lai Khe, dining at any one of Charlie Company's NDPs should have rated a Michelin star. Hats off to our cooks.

When there was really nothing going on around the base camp, some of us had an informal literary circle. The army occasionally sent us boxes of paperbacks, some of them quite good. My lieutenants and I would devour novels like Tolkien's *Lord of the Rings* trilogy, passed around among ourselves. A pure figment of imagination, Frodo's Middle Earth still had plenty of heroic excitement, sinister forces and credible leaders guided by transcendant values.

One welcome diversion from the war was the arrival of the Bob Hope Show during the year-end holiday. Some lucky enlisted men from each unit were transported to the big travelling show, which included top Stateside entertainment, screen starlets, *Playboy* models and Hope's own comedy.

One markedly futile fad in the bases was arson. Word came down the command chain to deny the enemy cover by torching the surrounding woods. Old tires were recomended as fire starters. We soon learned that the humid tropical forest was surprisingly fireproof, even in the dry monsoon. Smokey the Bear would be pleased to know that not even napalm and white phosphorous could keep a blaze going for long.

The GI experience in Vietnam can be distilled down to long stretches of boredom punctuated now and then by brief bursts of terror. Watching the sun set behind the forest outside Thunder IV one quiet evening made the war seem almost unreal. It was the stillness of twilight when light and dark call a truce – a private moment of contentment that invites contemplation.

We had adequate food, water, clothing and shelter, without money changing hands. The air we breathed was clean, the nature around us almost intact. And we shared loyalty, solidarity, comradery and purpose. When a man is lucky enough to have those essentials, should he still strive for more?

It's a rare soldier who didn't long for home. Most would return to seek out a niche in a vastly more complex and hectic way of life. And some would find themselves among the millions of our countrymen who had to struggle daily just to get the basic things we already had. Would all these men of our encampment really wind up happier, I wondered, than the simple Asian rice farmers in quaint conical hats that they were glad to put behind them?

–

„Charlie Six" and his company command track #306

Captain Edward Roby, NDP Lorraine II,
operation Shenandoah II, October 1967

Lai Khe, HQ Company C, 2/2 Infantry (Mech)
L-R: Sp4 Reynolds, Capt. Roby, Sgt. Boler.

Sources: all snapshots taken by member(s) of
Company C, names now unknown

after an 11-ton M-113 hits a mine...

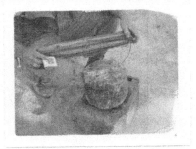

... such as this homemade explosive device

95

Chapter 16

Staff Doldrums

At Lai Khe, brigade and division staff officers below field grade were billeted in a partly open wooden barrack with walls of planks below wire mesh for air circulation. Known as the "Captains' Villa", the building was shaded by big trees in the northern part of the base, not far from the headquarters complex. This was my new home from May through mid-September.

Our neighbors here were the Vietnamese civilians of Lai Khe Village, a zoo-like wire-gated community so close to us that one could toss a stone into it – or a grenade out of it. I often wondered whether this spatial arrangement was a good idea.

There were about 30 fairly comfortable bunks in this quiet billets, each equipped with partly torn mosquito netting. Most bunks were empty and I rarely met the other resident officers, who were mostly coming or going on different working schedules around the clock.

Returning from one of my shifts at the brigade's tactical operations center (TOC) during the rainy summer monsoon, I froze in my tracks as I approached my bunk. Resting there on the middle of my blanket was a human skull. Holy Mackerel, I thought, What could I have done to offend the VC?

Like all the Jolly Roger skulls depicted on pirate flags, in horror comics or the movies. this pale white presence grinned sardonically through partly missing teeth. Upon cautious examination, though, the skull looked more like a doctor's anatomical specimen than a recent war trophy. It lacked the telltale bullet hole.

Nevertheless, I slept fitfully that night, wondering whether my sinister guest was some evil omen of impending death. After breakfast at the mess hall, I returned to the company of live men at the TOC. This operations center was now a fortified underground bunker with giant maps and banks of radios or cryptographic communications equipment covering the walls.

The TOC had moved out of the elegant French plantation building right next to us when rocket and mortar attacks became a daily menace.

I made the mistake of mentioning the mysterious skull that was still on my mind. A couple of lieutenants, one of them a former platoon leader of mine, listened politely. I was, after all, the assistant brigade operations officer, Duty Three Fox, their superior.

The conspiracy theory of belated VC revenge finally broke the ice with peals of raucous laughter. My former Charlie One Six, now an occasional chess partner, then sheepishly took credit for staging the prank with the skull. I might not have laughed quite as much as the others, but I sure was relieved.

The TOC bunker was almost sound proof. One day there was yet another rocket attack. The division engineer unit immediately called in to say their compound was taking big hits. What kind of incoming? I inquired. An unfamiliar voice broke into our radio transmission with perfect timing. "Da kine dat go Boom, BOOM, GI," the cheery VC net-crasher cackled.

So much for Lai Khe's audio communication security. The bunker's routine operations resumed in earnest only after our subterranean crew shook off recurring spasms of knee-slapping laughter. The targeted engineers could not have been amused but the brigade TOC at least appreciated that our opponents were not without an explosive sense of humor.

Red lines, Green tracers

The more glamorous part of my staff duty usually played out far above ground. When a major combat operation got underway or a big gunfight broke out in our brigade AO, the brigade operations officer, S3, would rush to his helicopter. As his assistant I went along, usually holding the maps or making the radio connections for the S3. This talented artillery major enjoyed his job and performed like a virtuoso. I learned the trade from watching him in action.

Whenever a decision is taken to support our maneuvering units on the ground with artillery or air strikes, it's crucial to make sure the supporting fires strike the enemy force without harming our own men. That's mainly the responsibility of the commanders of the ground troops and their forward air controllers or artillery forward observers who communicate with the jet pilots and firing batteries. But miscalculation entailed risk. Our artillery could bring down a jet fighter – or other high-fliers like our own Huey helicopter.

It could be likened to three-dimensional chess. The trick is to draw an imaginary horizontal line across the battlefield, safely separating our artillery's trajectory from the flight path of the jet fighters working the same target. And the best place to do that was our S3 chopper flying about a mile above the battle. If the enemy lacked anti-aircraft machine guns, we could risk dropping down to about 2,500 feet or less. It was a bit of a thrill to see small-arms tracers coming up to meet us. My boss thrived on it. Most of my 50 combat air hours were logged in the sky with him*.

One summer battle that got us off the ground took place southeast of Lai Khe. It involved an Australian regiment temporarily under the control of our brigade. Like every other maneuver element in the First Infantry Division, the Aussies were required immediately to fortify their new encampment before going to sleep. My job was to take status reports on their progress in digging foxholes and stringing barbed wire barriers. "Hey mate, we know how to take care of ourselves," was the cocky reply from our ally. Digging holes was clearly beneath them.

That bravado promptly boomerranged. They were attacked and partly overrun that night by a well-armed enemy force, an action that spilled into the next day and required air and artillery support. There were several casualties. Days later, a few of the Aussies swaggered over to visit Lai Khe, especially our club bars. They wore big brimmed outback hats and black scarves. There were a few curley-haired Aboriginal soldiers among them. Talk turned to sports, where teenage talent extraordinaire Yvonne Goolagong was just starting to garner attention. She soon became my favorite starlet on the women' tennis circuit on her way to world rank No. 1. My guess is that even the Aussies went home with a new respect for the VC/NVA and the value of stout fortifications.

Courtesy of the Army's gratis literary selections, I got hold of Ken Kesey's tragic-comic bestseller *One Flew Over the Cuckoo's Nest* that summer. And lo, a few of the madcap antics in the novel's locked-down

98

psychiatric clinic reminded me here and there of military foibles I'd observed in recent months.

The vibrant hub of social life in Lai Khe was the steambath. Soldiers in from the field found this a perfect place to relax and forget the war. It was also an exotic introduction to oriental culture almost unknown in their hometowns. Mama-san's steambath was also staffed by comely young massueses, some of whom were delighted to deploy other skills if the price was right.

There were three competing currencies: the Yankee dollar, the Vietnamese dong and the Army's scrip. Denominated in various paper notes bearing pictures of U.S. screen actressess like Marylin Monroe, Ava Gardner or Dorothy Lamour, scrip was introduced on Army installations to suppress circulation of the greenback among Vietnamese civilians. The drawback was that issues of scrip were periodically replaced with new ones to thwart a black market exchange for dollars.

A new chief of staff was in charge of the base and its non-military facilities. He took his job seriously and the presence of the steambaths apparently offended his austere code of values. Despite mama-san's popularity among the officers and men and her active cultivation of warm inter-cultural relations, the current scrip issue was declared void and the steambaths were closed. Lai Khe became a duller place and I set aside my own plan to extend my tour for a further six months.

—

*As a major general, Edward Trobaugh later commanded the 82nd Airborne Division in the conquest of Grenada, a Caribbean intervention ordered by President Reagan and occasionally remembered as "Operation Flyspeck".

Chapter 17

The Conflict in Retrospect

In the spring of 1975, President Gerald Ford's motorcade travelled about 75 miles from the White House to bucolic Winchester, Virginia, where Ford formally announced the end of the Vietnam War, already a fait accompli. I attended this deliberately low-key gathering in a Shenandoah Valley farmer's sunny pasture in order to file my report on the historic moment for United Press International.

Six years later a foreign war correspondent published one of the few books that treated the conflict in its entirety – a 30-year colonial war in which the Vietnamese first fought off the fading French empire and then frustrated a vigorous new Western superpower. This book was unusually objective because it was the first to let the politicians and generals on both sides comment on the long struggle in their own words. UPI assigned me to review the book. This is what I found:

A new look at the Vietnam War that lets the generals and politicians speak for themselves

by Edward Roby (UPI archive 4 Nov. 1981)

WASHINGTON – Political analyses of the Vietnam conflict now abound and there is no longer any shortage of excellent books providing a subjective view from the small hell of an Indochina foxhole.

But Michael Maclear's *The Ten Thousand Day War, Vietnam: 1945-1975* ($16.95 from St. Martin's Press, N.Y.C.) is unique. No other book in the growing literature on America's longest, most disastrous military adventure offers so complete and objective a glimpse within the command posts of both Washington and Hanoi.

Written by a British-born war correspondent for Canadian television, the book is an oral history, a mosaic of first-person interviews by Maclear and a few other journalists with the politicians and generals who gave us the Vietnam War.

The leaders speak for themselves, taking turns in a smooth, journalistic narrative that Maclear serves up in chronological order from the Japanese surrender of Hanoi through Dien Bien Phu, the Gulf of Tonkin resolution, Khe Sanh and Hamburger Hill to the fall of Saigon.

They are all there: five U.S. presidents, Ho Chi Minh, Robert McNamara, Vo Nguyen Giap, William Westmoreland, Le Duc Tho, Henry Kissinger, Ngo Dinh Diem, Henry Cabot Lodge, Nguyen Van Thieu, Alexander Haig, William Colby, the Bundy brothers, Dean Rusk and dozens more.

Lies and deceptions bob to the surface as they offer warring versions of events in their own words. It's up to the reader to decide who is right, for Maclear does not comment.

"This is the importance of the book – that it brought all these political figures together for the first time," says the author. "I think the story of Vietnam was essentially the story of how Americans were kept in the dark."

Lyndon Johnson, for instance, publicly insists his bombers hit only military targets as entire Vietnamese cities are flattened. And CIA chief William Colby states none of Hanoi's troops were operating in the South when Johnson approved the bombing, ostensibly as retaliation.

Maclear shows how America's objective in Vietnam was as elusive as the enemy it found there.

"It was startling for me to find out that we had no military plan to win the war," confides Clark Clifford as he took over the Pentagon post from a distraught Robert McNamara on the eve of the 1968 Tet offensive.

President Franklin Roosevelt, who spoke of freeing the colonial peoples, sent the first OSS men to make common cause with Ho's Viet Minh against the occupying Japanese during World War II.

But France was permitted to reclaim its Asian empire and Washington helped Paris battle the Viet Minh until the Dien Bien Phu debacle. France lost 74,000 men in seven years combat before the 1954 Geneva accords.

Dwight Eisenhower, who feared Ho would be acclaimed leader of a unified Vietnam under the terms of the accords, conspired to thwart free elections in the South and backed a Catholic mandarin called Diem.

When Diem's corruption, nepotism, rigged elections and brutal repression of political foes and the majority Buddhists became too much, President John Kennedy fomented a generals' coup but professed shock at the bloody outcome. In the chaos of military juntas that followed, Kennedy seemed ready to cut U.S. losses and get out when he himself was slain.

Johnson, an early Vietnam dove who inherited hawkish advisers, was soon pursuaded to risk U.S. troops. But when thousands of them came home in body bags, his presidency and his dreams of The Great Society crumbled.

President Richard Nixon, who promised a secret plan to end the war, prolonged it with four years of tedious negotiations, furious carpet bombings, unravelling troop morale and domestic anti-war riots.

"Peace with honor" became a new rationale for further bloodshed after the Sino-Soviet rift showed there was no Communist monolith to stop at the 17th parallel. Toward the end, the justification seemed to be simply macho.

"It wasn't until 1968, the Tet offensive, that the war became any great public issue," says Maclear. By then, Gen. Westmoreland had already been feted as *Time's* man of the year.

Maclear believes television news is creating a "unique interaction between the battle front and the home front. TV altered the nature of war from now on," he says.

In fact, his account of television's first war is essentially a spinoff from a 26-part television documentary of the same name that is to be aired in coming months. But it contains perhaps 100 times as much material as the film version.

It's ironic that one thing television might have shown best – the awesome bombing of North Vietnam – was never really seen by the American public.

A trip north of the 18th parallel just after the 1969 bombing halt revealed a moonscape of hundreds of shattered villages, towns and cities, Maclear writes.

"Across the whole landscape, journeying far from the highway, not a single habitable brick edifice could be seen: the schools, hospitals and administrative buildings that had certainly once existed were now, like the factories, just so many heaps of rubble."

The mayor of Ha Tinh, once a large provincial capital 250 miles from Hanoi, documented 25,529 bombings between 1965 and 1968 -- an air strike every 90 minutes. The city hospital with 170 persons and its secondary school with 750 pupils were destroyed in the initial air assault, later described as "a conscious massacre."

The Vietnamese say 20 cameramen died filming the four-year bombing of Vinh Linh, a city that absorbed three times the explosive tonnage as Japan in World War II.

Those that survived Rolling Thunder, as the constant, random air and sea bombardment was known, resumed their lives again underground.

"Children born below the earth ... were carefully exposed to the sun for a few minutes each day," Maclear writes. The unprecedented blitz was supposed to crush all will to resist within six months of its 1964 inception.

It lasted seven times as long, and the gathering weight of evidence showed it counterproductive.

Rather than cracking enemy morale, it helped unify the country in cooperation for survival.

"Each sector or 'village' had its clinic, school, nursery and recreational center, and, as in the age before the bombers, tended to its own fields and communal affairs," Maclear writes.

Some 182,000 civilians had died at a rate of 1,000 a week by November 1968, according to an estimate by McNamara, architect of the bombing campaign that apparently preyed on his conscience.

Both the Johnson and Nixon administrations eventually realized bombing would not win the war. But they clung to the idea that Hanoi's leaders, by all accounts rock-stable, would seek political compromise.

A McNamara memo published in the Pentagon Papers warned: "There may be a limit beyond which many Americans and much of the world will not permit the United States to go. The picture of the world's greatest superpower killing or seriously injuring 1,000 non-combatants a week, while trying to pound a tiny backward nation into submission on an issue whose merits are hotly disputed, is not a pretty one." And the Nixon 1972 Christmas bombings of Hanoi and Haiphong were more vicious. But the peace settlement Kissinger and Le Duc Tho initialled in Paris on Jan. 23, 1973, was the same one they had agreed on the previous October.

In the South, forests and rubber plantations fell before Rome plows or were killed by defoliants sprayed willy-nilly. Bombs and shells rained on so-called free-fire zones where villages were razed to keep them out of guerrilla hands although families still hid in the woods.

We are left with mere statistical hints of the carnage, which Vietnam's U.N. Ambassador, Ha Van Lau, put at "as many as 15 million dead and wounded" in the decades of war after the 1958 Geneva deadline for Vietnam's reunification.

The American people, who debated the impact of the Tet offensive, the endless peace talks and the Belsen-like body-strewn ditches of My Lai, still know little of the bombings – their country's forte in modern warfare.

The United States, which lost some 57,000 men in combat, or about as many as in World War I, paid a profound political price. The undeclared war spotlighted the limits of power more than its arrogance.

South Vietnam was abandoned after being cast as a vital bastion of the Free World. President Thieu called it betrayal.

President Nixon, who reached a historic understanding with China, spread war to Cambodia to give a bizarre new life to the discredited domino theory. America tarnished its image by slipping smoothly into the role of the vanquished French in a misguided colonial adventure it had once condemned.

And the U.S. government squandered a deep reservoir of public trust, alienating large groups, aggravating social problems and saddling today's leaders with credibility problems in the conduct of foreign policy.

The distasteful images – My Lai, tiger cages, terrorism, repression, torture, corruption, surgical bombings, coups, assassinations, concentration camps, bloody combat and villages destroyed in order to save them – all took a toll on the American psyche.

The Vietnam peace marches, draft resistance and civil disobedience, culminating with the shootings at Kent State University, prompted one seasoned observer to wonder whether America was still governable.

Nowhere were strains more apparent than in the plunging morale – the mutinies, defections and fraggings – of the conscript force sent to fight for a dying cause 12,000 miles from home.

"What we thought was the spread of Communist aggression in my opinion now seems very clearly to have been a civil war in Vietnam," observes Clifford, the former hawk.

But Gen. Haig says he's "always felt that this was more of an East-West issue." And President Reagan, Haig's new boss, now regards the conflict "a noble cause."

–

Glossary

AK-47: standard rifle of Viet Cong and North Vietnamese soldiers

AO: area of operations

Ap: Vienamese for a village, e.g. Ap Bo La, Ap Bau Bang

APC: armored personnel carrier, M-113. Also called PC, A-Cav, track

ARVN: Army of the Republic of Vietnam (South Vietnam)

ASAP: acronym for "as soon as possible"

AWOL: acronym for "absent without leave"

battalion: infantry unit composed of about 650 soldiers, divided into companies; armored cavalry equivalent is called a squadron

Big Red One: nickname for the First Infantry Division, its ensignia bearing a large Arabic numeral 1 colored red.

brigade: combat command echelon of an infantry division to which battalions are assigned ad hoc to accomplish specific missions; a division usually has three such brigades

C4: plastic explosive for demolitions

C&C: command and control helicopter

CG: commanding general (division or higher)

check fire: command to desist from shooting

CO: commanding officer (any unit)

company: infantry unit composed of 150-200 soldiers, divided into three mechanized platoons or four platoons of foot soldiers in light infantry. In armored cavalry, the equivalent is called a troop.

CP: command post

CPT: captain (rank of a company's CO), also Capt.

C-rations: U.S. field rations issued to each soldier

dai uy: Vietnamese word for captain

division: infantry unit composed of about 16,000 soldiers divided into maneuver battalions and various supporting units

dust-off: medical evacuation by helicopter

EMs: enlisted men (privates, PFC/privates first class, Sp/specialists and NCOs)

EOD: Explosive ordnance disposal; special unit that does this

fire base: fortified field base with an artillery battery

first sergeant: a company's ranking non-commissioned officer, nickname: Top

FO: forward observer, usually an artillery lieutenant who accompanies a maneuvering unit's command group as liaison with batteries firing in support.

GI: nickname for a U.S. soldier; acronym for "government issue"

heavy machine gun: .50 caliber gun pintel-mounted on M-113s; range: five miles

H&I fires: Harassment and interdiction; shelling of free-fire zones

Huey: UH-1 helicopter

KIA: killed in action

light infantry: in this text, units of foot soldiers; also called leg infantry or straight infantry to distinguish from mechanized infantry

LP: listening post

LRP: long range patrol

LRRP: long range reconnaissance patrol

LT or Lt.: designates rank of "lieutenant". 1Lt = first lieutenant; 2Lt = second lieutenant

LTC: lieutenant colonel (rank of a battalion commander)

LTG: lieutenant general (three-star general seen only in units above division)

LZ: landing zone; place where troop-carrying helicopters land infantry soldiers; "hot" LZ if contested

M-16: standard U.S. rifle (5.56-mm) for infantry soldiers; short-barrelled, lighter, carbine version is called AR-15.

M-60: standard U.S. light machine gun (7.62-mm)

M-79: U.S. (40-mm) grenade launcher

Maj.: abbreviates rank of major, one grade above captain

meter: metric measure used in the military; one meter = 3.28084 feet or roughly a yard

MG: major general (rank of a division comander, who has two brigadier generals as deputies)

mechanized infantry: units that can move on foot or mounted on vehicles; armored infantry; also called mech

mortar: tube-like indirect-fire weapon that fires projectiles in high trajectory; range can exceed three miles for 81-mm mortar

napalm: incendary mixture of thickened petroleum dropped in canisters by aircraft

NCO: non-commissioned officer (sergeant or corporal)

NDP: night defensive position

NVA: North Vietnamese Army

phonetic alphabet: Alpha, Bravo, Charlie, Delta, Echo ... X-Ray, Yankee, Zulu (substitutes for letters to enhance clarity in communications)

platoon: infantry formation with 45-50 soldiers, divided into squads

point man: lead soldier in an advancing infantry file or column

radio call-signs: "Six", prefaced by the battalion, company or platoon radio name, was reserved for the commanding officer of that unit, e.g. Daring Six for the CO of the 2/2, Alpha Six for the CO of any battalion's Company A, or Three Six, the platoon leader of any company's Third Platoon. "Five" designated the executive officer/XO of any such unit, e.g. Charlie Five, XO of Company C.

regiment: now an historic echelon with which subordinate battalions are traditionally still identified for heraldic purposes. E.g. the First Infantry Division had two battalions of the Second Infantry Regiment, namely the 1st Battalion (light infantry) and the 2nd Battalion (mechanized infantry).

RPG: enemy's rocket-propelled grenade and launcher with projectiles including B-40 shaped charges or airbursts, e.g. RPG-2, RPG-7, B-40

R & R: acronym for rest and recreation; a one-time five-day leave from the war, usually outside Vietnam

RTO: radio telephone operator (soldier with multi-frequency radio in a unit's command group)

S-3: the staff officer for tactical operations of a brigade or battalion (usually a major); other staff positions are S-1 for personnel, S-2 for intelligence, S-4 for logistics

SITREP: situation report

Song: Vietnamese for river, e.g. Song Be, Song Dong Nai, Song Saigon

squad: infantry formation with 9 to 11 men, divided into two fire teams

The Old Man: nickname for a company commander, usually a captain; relict of times when promotion was slow and the CO might no longer be young.

TOC: tactical operations center (of a brigade headquarters or higher)

Viet Cong: the organized enemy insurgents in South Vietnam

WIA: wounded in action

WP: white phosphorous, often called Willy Peter

XO: executive officer, next in command to the unit's CO.